William C. Green

The Plutus of Aristophanes

William C. Green

The Plutus of Aristophanes

ISBN/EAN: 9783337038410

Printed in Europe, USA, Canada, Australia, Japan

Cover: Foto ©Thomas Meinert / pixelio.de

More available books at **www.hansebooks.com**

𝕻𝖎𝖙𝖙 𝕻𝖗𝖊𝖘𝖘 𝕾𝖊𝖗𝖎𝖊𝖘.

THE

PLUTUS OF ARISTOPHANES

BY

W. C. GREEN, M.A.

RECTOR OF HEPWORTH, SUFFOLK;
LATE FELLOW OF KING'S COLLEGE, CAMBRIDGE;
AND ASSISTANT MASTER AT RUGBY SCHOOL.

New Edition, revised and corrected.

EDITED FOR THE SYNDICS OF THE UNIVERSITY PRESS.

𝕮𝖆𝖒𝖇𝖗𝖎𝖉𝖌𝖊 :

AT THE UNIVERSITY PRESS

1892

INTRODUCTION TO THE PLUTUS.

THE *Plutus* was exhibited in the archonship of Antipater, that is to say B.C. 388 ; being the last play that Aristophanes produced in his own name. For his two remaining plays, the *Aeolosicon* and *Cocalus*, were put forth through Araros one of his sons, whom he wished thus to introduce to the Athenian public.

Thus much we learn from the writer of one of the Greek arguments. But a Scholiast tells us that there were two plays of Aristophanes bearing this name; and that the first *Plutus* was exhibited in the archonship of Diocles (B.C. 408). From this first *Plutus* a line (not in our play) is quoted by the Scholiast on *Ran.* 1093 : on l. 115 of our play the Scholiast gives an alteration made (as he says) in the second *Plutus;* and lines 173, 1146 are noticed as necessarily belonging to the later play. This Scholiast evidently supposes the play which he is annotating to be substantially the first *Plutus;* into which lines 173, 1146, which must belong to the later play, have been transferred.

But the more general and better conclusion is that the play which we have is the second *Plutus.* The whole character of the play, the absence of choric interludes and personalities, are a mark of the later time : the historical references are thus correct and natural. Indeed there is nothing of which we could positively assert that it was not in the second *Plutus.* For though in lines 174, 303, 314 persons are mentioned by name, they are of no great note, we are not sure that they were still living, nor is the satire on them so bitter that it must have provoked the penalty of the law against personalities. Or, if some few lines be thought to have belonged to the earlier, but probably not to the later play, they may as easily have been in-

serted by copyists remembering the earlier play as *vice versa*.
And if there be any truth in the proverb that 'second thoughts
are best' we shall surely judge our line 115 ταύτης ἀπαλλάξειν
σε τῆς ὀφθαλμίας to be later than the weak substitute given by
the Scholiast τῆς συμφορᾶς ταύτης σε παύσειν ἧς ἔχεις.

Be it then assumed that our *Plutus* is the later play : 'a
refashionment of an earlier work of Aristophanes,' as Donaldson
calls it : though how far the two plays differed we do not know ;
they may have been substantially the same.

It appears however nearly certain that there were interludes
of the Chorus in the *First Plutus*, which we have not in ours :
and in such parts and elsewhere there was probably personal
satire which in the later edition was omitted. For we know
that the licence of Comedy had now been abridged by law : as
Horace says, 'Chorus turpiter obticuit sublato jure nocendi.'
In fact the *Plutus*, with the *Ecclesiazusae*, belongs to what
Meineke calls the third age of Aristophanic poetry. Athens was
conquered and humbled by the issue of the Peloponnesian war.
Her leading position and liberty were lost. Comedy, as Aristophanes had originally conceived it—where the comic poet was
to be the frank and fearless adviser of the State, reprover of
mistaken policy, exposer of trickery and vice even in high
places, roundly abusing his countrymen for their own good (see
the Parabasis of the *Acharnians*)—comedy of this kind could
no longer exist. With the greatness of the country had fallen
the greatness of the poet's office. Not only by law was the
Chorus silenced or restricted ; but also poverty in place of
wealth made it impossible to put plays on the stage with the old
splendour. Aristophanes therefore of necessity conforms to the
times : and though there are sparkles of his old wit, the general
character of language is tamer. With the old bitterness is gone
much of the old vigour.

The *Plutus* therefore may be ranked as belonging to Middle
Comedy (if there be any definite Middle Comedy); at all events
to the time of transition from the Old to the New. It deals not
with political but private life : with the general question of the
distribution of riches in the world, with the question whether

riches or poverty do most good. This question is solved by bringing on the stage the god of Wealth, restoring him to sight, and describing the consequences, when riches were now redistributed according to his and Chremylus' ideas of merit. For a sketch of the play one can hardly do better than reproduce that given by Addison in No. 464 of *The Spectator.* He calls it 'a very pretty allegory which is wrought into a play by Aristophanes the Greek Comedian.'

'Chremylus, who was an old and a good man, and withal exceeding poor, being desirous to leave some riches to his son, consults the oracle of Apollo upon the subject. The oracle bid him follow the first man he should see upon his going out of the temple. The person he chanced to see was to appearance an old sordid blind man, but, upon his following him from place to place, he at last found, by his own confession, that he was Plutus the god of riches, and that he was just come out of the house of a miser. Plutus further told him that when he was a boy he used to declare that as soon as he came to age he would distribute wealth to none but virtuous and just men; upon which Jupiter, considering the pernicious consequences of such a resolution, took his sight away from him, and left him to stroll about the world in the blind condition wherein Chremylus beheld him. With much ado Chremylus prevailed upon him to go to his house; where he met an old woman in a tattered raiment, who had been his guest for many years, and whose name was Poverty. The old woman refusing to turn out so easily as he would have her, he threatened to banish her, not only from his house, but out of all Greece, if she made any more words upon the matter. Poverty on this occasion pleads her cause very notably, and represents to her old landlord that, should she be driven out of the country, all their trades arts and sciences would be driven out with her; and that, if every one was rich, they would never be supplied with those pomps, ornaments and conveniences of life which make riches desirable. She likewise represented to him the several advantages which she bestowed upon her votaries, in regard to their shape, their health, and their activity, by preserving them from gouts, dropsies, unwieldiness and intemperance; but whatever she had to say for herself she was at last forced to troop off. Chremylus immediately considered how he might restore Plutus to his sight; and in order to it, conveyed him to the temple of Aesculapius, who was famous for cures and miracles of this nature. By this means the deity recovered his eyes, and began to make a right use of them, by enriching every one that was distinguished by piety towards the gods and justice towards men; and at the same time by taking away his gifts from the impious and undeserving. This produces several merry incidents, till, in the very last act, Mercury descends with great complaints from the gods that, since the good men were grown rich, they had received no sacrifices; which is confirmed by a priest of Jupiter, who enters with a remonstrance that since the late innovation he was reduced to a starving condition, and could not live upon his office. Chremylus, who in the beginning of the play was religious in his poverty, concludes it with a proposal, which was relished by all the good men who were now grown rich as well as himself, that they should carry Plutus in a solemn procession to the temple, and instal him in the place of Jupiter.'

'This allegory instructed the Athenians in two points; first, as it vindicated the conduct of Providence in its ordinary distributions of wealth; and, in the next place, as it showed the great tendency of riches to corrupt the morals of those who possessed them.'

While appreciating Addison's elegant sketch of the allegory, we shall not entirely agree with him as to its drift : the lesson intended by Aristophanes cannot have been exactly as he says.

In the first place, Aristophanes cannot have meant to show that the distribution of wealth at Athens was the best possible, or that it was absolutely better for good and honest men to be poor. We cannot suppose that the restoration of Plutus to sight and the re-distribution of riches by merit—i.e. the whole action of the play—is meant to be an elaborate mistake. From the analogy of all his plays our poet must be believed, in the main, to sympathize with those who are victorious in the end.

For instance, in the *Peace* the recovery of the goddess Peace was really to the poet, as well as to his characters, a desired end: so also in the *Acharnians* the truce, in the *Frogs* the return of Aeschylus. Therefore in this play that toward which the main action is directed, giving sight to Plutus, must be a wish of the poet as well as of Chremylus. One cannot doubt that Aristophanes meant not to approve, but to complain of, the present distribution of riches, at least at Athens that he thought they fell to the undeserving: that he meant a sort of regretful lament over old times when better men prospered.

And secondly, as regards the comparative effects of riches and poverty, though he admires the thrift and hardy virtue of old times as contrasted with the corruptions of luxury, yet he would naturally defend plenty and wealth; for he would regard them as characteristics of the old times, and as an indispensable aid to old Comedy, in contrast with the present humiliation of his country and the degradation of the comic poet's office. The two lessons therefore of the allegory are not simply 'the vindication of Providence in its ordinary distributions of wealth' and 'the tendency of riches to corrupt.' At the same time we may own that these two lessons do in some sort appear, at least to us. The whole impression left on us is not that Plutus' recovery is a signal success. Though certain impostors and worthless fellows are disgraced, no very noble results seem likely to follow. And again, Poverty in her pleading with Chremylus has undoubtedly the best of the argument: indeed Chremylus can only end by saying that 'he wo'nt be convinced' (l. 600). And it was inevitable that Aristophanes, in working out these arguments, should see that poverty was the spur to exertion, that unequal distribution of wealth was a good and necessary thing. But in behalf of Wealth, and against Poverty, it might have been argued with some force that men work to win wealth as much as to escape poverty; that, where some must win, it would be better that the winners should be the worthier. But that men are made worthier by having to work in order to win, while the very fact of having won wealth often tends to make them less worthy, is a truth to which Aristophanes was not blind; and still less can we be so. Work done on the way to an end is often more valuable to the worker than the end itself. But after all we are not concerned to prove Aristophanes absolutely consistent, or the allegory of the *Plutus* perfect. The poet saw many anomalies, and much unfairness, in the distribution of wealth at Athens in his time. These he wished to point out, and, in imagination, to set matters to rights. An amusing way of doing so seemed to be by restoring to sight Plutus, proverbially blind. Some of the real advantages and uses of poverty are brought out by the way; and the results of Plutus' and Chremylus' new arrangements are not very grand: for Chremylus is no very high type of character, nor intended by Aristophanes to be so. But the idea gave opportunity (as Addison says) 'for many merry incidents': and we must not forget that to amuse—always one chief object of comedy—was now more than ever so, when serious personal satire and political teaching was no longer possible.

Meineke notices that 'in this play throughout the gods are severely handled, so that we can perceive that the old reverence for them had passed away, even among men with pretensions to goodness.' There is much ridicule of the gods also in the *Frogs* and *Birds*, though in a playful vein. Yet it is rather the tricks of priestcraft and superstition (which may have been gaining ground) than the serious part of religion that our poet attacks. Zeus indeed is made to give place to Plutus at the end of the play: but then the priest of Zeus has already lowered his deity by representing him as only anxious for his perquisites. We need not blame Aristophanes over much for seeing through and exposing the impostures and absurdities of his national theology.

The *Plutus* has a more copious body of Scholia than any other play of Aristophanes; and (as a consequence probably of this) has been very fully annotated by the learned scholars of old. The actual difficulties of the play, whether of language or allusion, do not need long notes. And as to its interest and merit most will now agree with Meineke in classing it far below our poet's earlier plays.

TABLE OF THE READINGS OF DINDORF'S AND MEINEKE'S TEXTS.

	DINDORF.	MEINEKE.
17.	ἀποκρινομένῳ	ἀποκρινόμενος
37.	μηδὲ ἕν	μηδεέν
45.	ξυνίῃς	ξυνιεῖς
46.	φράζουσαν	φράζοντος
49.	συμφέρον	σύμφορον
56.	πρότερον...φράσον	πότερον...φράσεις
78-79.	ΧΡ. ὤ...Πλοῦτος ὤν	ΚΑ. ὤ...Πλοῦτος ὤν
80.	ΚΑ. σὺ Πλοῦτος	ΧΡ. σὺ Πλοῦτος
81.	ΧΡ. ὤ Φοῖβ᾽ Ἄπcλλον	Chremyli est
98.	ἑόρακά πω	ἑόρακ᾽ ἐγὼ
105.	ἐμέλλετον	ἐμελλέτην
130.	τίν᾽	τί
162-167.	Chremyli sunt	Chremyli et Carionis sunt alternis
170-179.	Carionis sunt	Chremyli et Carionis sunt alternis
197.	αὐτῷ	εἶναι
208.	μὴ νῦν	μή νυν
211.	δρᾶσαι	δρᾶν σὺ
217.	κἂν δῇ	κἂν χρῇ
237.	εἰς	ὡς
244.	χρόνῳ	χρόνου
258.	ἄνδρας	ὄντας
271.	ἡμᾶς	μ᾽ ἔπειτ᾽
286.	ἄπασιν ἡμῖν	ἡμῖν ἄπασιν
287.	Μίδας	Μίδαις
296.	γ᾽ αὖ	γε
301.	σφηκίσκον	σφηνίσκον
335.	τί ἂν οὖν τὸ πρᾶγμ᾽ εἴη; πόθεν	τί τὸ πρᾶγμ᾽ ἂν εἴη καὶ πόθεν ;
338.	ἐπί	ἐν
361.	τοιοῦτο. ΒΛ. φεῦ	τοιουτονί
362.	ὡς	ΒΛ. φεῦ· ὡς

	DINDORF.	MEINEKE.
368.	ἐπίδηλόν τι πεπανουργηκότι	ἐπίδηλον ὅτι πεπανούργηκέ τι
375.	ἐθέλεις	ἐθέλει
406.	εἰσαγαγεῖν	εἰσάγειν
413.	ἄννε	ἄνυτε
485.	φθάνοιτον	φθάνοιτε
	πράττοντ'· ἢ τί γὰρ	πράττοντες· τί γὰρ
493.	βούλημα	βούλευμα
498.	τίς	τὶς
499.	οὐδεὶς ἄν· ἐγὼ	οὐδέν· ἐγώ σοι
505.	παῦσαι	παύσει
506.	ἤντιν'	ἤν τις
517.	νῦν δὴ	νυνὶ
521.	παρὰ πλείστων	παρ' ἀπίστων
531.	ἐστιν	ἔσται
536.	κολοσυρτόν	κολοσυρτοῦ
545.	θράνους	θράνου
548.	ὑπεκρούσω	ἐπικρούσω
573.	ἀναπείσειν	ἀναπείθειν
582.	σὲ διδάξω	ἀποδείξω
584.	ἵν' Ἕλληνας...ξυναγείρει	omittit
587.	δηλοῖ	δῆλος
592.	κοτινῷ	κοτίνῳ
607.	χρή	χρῆν
	ἀνύειν	ἀνύτειν
630.	ἄλλοι	ἄλλοι
661.	προθύματα	θυλήματα
669.	παρήγγειλεν καθεύδειν	παρήγγειλ' ἐγκαθεύδειν
689.	τὴν χεῖρ' ὑφῄρει	ἄρασ' ὑφῄρει
725.	ἐπομνύμενον	ὑπομνύμενον
	τῆς ἐκκλησίας	ταῖς ἐκκλησίαις
738.	ἀνεστήκει	ἀνειστήκει
770.	ἀπαντῆσαι	ὑπαντῆσαι
781.	ἐνεδίδουν	ἐπεδίδουν
801.	τὰς ἰσχάδας	τῶν ἰσχάδων
813.	σαπροὺς	σαθροὺς
839.	μ' ἀπώλεσεν	σ' ἀπώλεσεν mutata persona
840.	ΧΡ. ἀλλ' οὐχὶ νῦν. ΔΙ. ἀνθ' ὧν	ΔΙ. ἀλλ' οὐχὶ νῦν. ἀνθ' ὧν

DINDORF.	MEINEKE.
845. μῶν ἐνεμυνήθης	μῶν οὖν ἐμυήθης
870. οὐδενὸς	οὐδεέν
908. μαθών	παθών
919. ὥστ'	ὡς
946. καί	κᾶν
979. ταὐτὰ πάνθ'	γ' αὖ τὰ πάνθ'
993. οὐχὶ νῦν ἔθ'	οὐχί τοι νῦν
1004. ἔπειτα πλουτῶν	ἐπεὶ ξαπλουτῶν
1005. ἅπαντ' ἐπήσθιεν	ἅπαντ' ἂν ἤσθιεν
1010. λυπουμένην	λυπουμένην γ'
1011. φάττιον	φάβιον
1018. παγκάλους	παγκάλας
1027. ποιήσει	ποιήσῃ
1033. νυνδί σ' οὐκέτι	νῦν δέ γ' οὐκέτι σε
1037. τηλία	τηλίας
1042. τί	σέ
1055. πρός με	πρὸς ἐμὲ
ποῖ	ποῦ
1078. τοῦτό γ' ἐπέτρεπον	τοῦτ' ἐπέτρεψ' ἐγὼ
1100. ἆ	ὁ
1116. ἐπιθύει	ἔτι θύει
1131. πρὸς	περί
ἐπιστρέφειν	ἔτι στρέφειν
1139. τι	γε
1140. σε λανθάνειν	σ' ἂν λανθάνειν
1141. αὐτὸς	καὐτὸς
1171. φράσειε ποῦ	φράσει' ὅπου
1173. ὁ Πλοῦτος οὗτος ἤρξατο βλέπειν	αὖ βλέπειν ὁ Πλοῦτος ἤρξατο
1189. ἐνθάδε	ἐνθαδί

ΤΑ ΤΟΥ ΔΡΑΜΑΤΟΣ ΠΡΟΣΩΠΑ.

ΚΑΡΙΩΝ.
ΧΡΕΜΥΛΟΣ.
ΠΛΟΥΤΟΣ.
ΧΟΡΟΣ ΑΓΡΟΙΚΩΝ.
ΒΛΕΨΙΔΗΜΟΣ.
ΠΕΝΙΑ.
ΓΥΝΗ ΧΡΕΜΥΛΟΥ.
ΔΙΚΑΙΟΣ ΑΝΗΡ.
ΣΥΚΟΦΑΝΤΗΣ.
ΓΡΑΥΣ.
ΝΕΑΝΙΑΣ.
ΕΡΜΗΣ.
ΙΕΡΕΥΣ ΔΙΟΣ.

ΥΠΟΘΕΣΙΣ.

Βουλόμενος Ἀριστοφάνης σκῶψαι τοὺς Ἀθηναίους ἀδικίᾳ
καὶ συκοφαντίᾳ καὶ τοῖς τοιούτοις συνόντας, καὶ διὰ τοῦτο πλουτοῦντας, πλάττει πρεσβύτην τινὰ γεωργὸν Χρεμύλον τοὔνομα,
δίκαιον μὲν ὄντα καὶ τοὺς τρόπους χρηστόν, πένητα δὲ ἄλλως·
ὃς μετά τινος αὐτῷ θεράποντος ἐλθὼν εἰς Ἀπόλλω ἐρωτᾷ περὶ
τοῦ ἰδίου παιδός, εἰ χρὴ τουτονὶ τρόπων χρηστῶν ἀμελήσαντα
ἀδικίας ἀντιποιεῖσθαι καὶ ταὐτὰ τοῖς ἄλλοις ἐπιτηδεύειν, ἐπει-
δήπερ οἱ μὲν τοιοῦτοι ἐπλούτουν, οἱ δὲ τὰ ἀγαθὰ πράττοντες
πένητες ἦσαν, καθάπερ αὐτὸς οὗτος ὁ Χρεμύλος. ἔχρησεν οὖν
αὐτῷ ὁ θεὸς σαφὲς μὲν οὐδέν, ὅτῳ δὲ ἐξιὼν ἐντύχοι, τούτῳ ἕπεσθαι. καὶ ὃς γέροντι ἐντυγχάνει τυφλῷ, ἦν δὲ οὗτος ὁ Πλοῦτος,
καὶ ἀκολουθεῖ κατὰ τὰς μαντείας, μὴ εἰδὼς ὅτι ὁ Πλοῦτός ἐστι.
δυσχεραίνων δὲ ἐπὶ τούτῳ καθ᾽ ἑαυτὸν ὁ θεράπων μόλις αὐτὸν
ἐρωτᾷ τίνος ἕνεκα τούτῳ ἀκολουθοῦσι. καὶ ὁ Χρεμύλος λέγει
αὐτῷ τὴν μαντείαν. ἔπειτα μανθάνουσι παρ᾽ αὐτοῦ τοῦ Πλούτου
ὅστις ἐστὶ καὶ ὅτου χάριν τυφλὸς ἐγεγόνει παρὰ τοῦ Διός. οἱ
δὲ ἀκούσαντες ἥσθησάν τε καὶ βουλὴν ἐβουλεύσαντο ἀπαγαγεῖν
αὐτὸν εἰς Ἀσκληπιοῦ καὶ τὴν τῶν ὀφθαλμῶν θεραπεῦσαι πήρω-
σιν. καὶ ἵνα τὰ ἐν μέσῳ παρῶ, τάς τε τοῦ Βλεψιδήμου ἀντιλο-
γίας καὶ τῆς Πενίας αὐτῆς, ἀπήγαγόν τε αὐτὸν ὅ τι τάχιστα καὶ
ὑγιᾶ ἐπανήγαγον οἴκαδε, ἐπλούτησάν τε ἱκανῶς οὐκ αὐτοὶ μόνον,
ἀλλὰ καὶ ὅσοι βίου χρηστοῦ πρόσθεν ἀντεχόμενοι πένητες ἦσαν.

Ἐδιδάχθη ἐπὶ ἄρχοντος Ἀντιπάτρου, ἀνταγωνιζομένου αὐτῷ
Νικοχάρους μὲν Λάκωσιν, Ἀριστομένους δὲ Ἀδμήτῳ, Νικο-
φῶντος δὲ Ἀδώνιδι, Ἀλκαίου δὲ Πασιφάῃ. τελευταίαν δὲ
διδάξας τὴν κωμῳδίαν ταύτην ἐπὶ τῷ ἰδίῳ ὀνόματι, [καὶ] τὸν
υἱὸν αὐτοῦ συστῆσαι Ἀραρότα [δι᾽ αὐτῆς] τοῖς θεαταῖς βουλόμενος, τὰ ὑπόλοιπα δύο δι᾽ ἐκείνου καθῆκε, Κώκαλον καὶ
Αἰολοσίκωνα.

G. P.   I

ΠΛΟΥΤΟΣ.

ΚΑ. Ὡς ἀργαλέον πρᾶγμ᾽ ἐστὶν, ὦ Ζεῦ καὶ θεοὶ,
δοῦλον γενέσθαι παραφρονοῦντος δεσπότου.
ἢν γὰρ τὰ βέλτισθ᾽ ὁ θεράπων λέξας τύχῃ,
δόξῃ δὲ μὴ δρᾶν ταῦτα τῷ κεκτημένῳ,
μετέχειν ἀνάγκη τὸν θεράποντα τῶν κακῶν.   5
τοῦ σώματος γὰρ οὐκ ἐᾷ τὸν κύριον
κρατεῖν ὁ δαίμων, ἀλλὰ τὸν ἐωνημένον.
καὶ ταῦτα μὲν δὴ ταῦτα.   τῷ δὲ Λοξίᾳ,
ὃς θεσπιῳδεῖ τρίποδος ἐκ χρυσηλάτου,
μέμψιν δικαίαν μέμφομαι ταύτην, ὅτι   10
ἰατρὸς ὢν καὶ μάντις, ὥς φασιν, σοφὸς,
μελαγχολῶντ᾽ ἀπέπεμψέ μου τὸν δεσπότην,
ὅστις ἀκολουθεῖ κατόπιν ἀνθρώπου τυφλοῦ,
τοὐναντίον δρῶν ἢ προσῆκ᾽ αὐτῷ ποιεῖν.
οἱ γὰρ βλέποντες τοῖς τυφλοῖς ἡγούμεθα·   15
οὗτος δ᾽ ἀκολουθεῖ, κἀμὲ προσβιάζεται,
καὶ ταῦτ᾽ ἀποκρινομένῳ τὸ παράπαν οὐδὲ γρῦ.
ἐγὼ μὲν οὖν οὐκ ἔσθ᾽ ὅπως σιγήσομαι,
ἢν μὴ φράσῃς ὅ τι τῷδ᾽ ἀκολουθοῦμέν ποτε,
ὦ δέσποτ᾽, ἀλλά σοι παρέξω πράγματα.   20
οὐ γάρ με τυπτήσεις στέφανον ἔχοντά γε.
ΧΡ. μὰ Δί᾽, ἀλλ᾽ ἀφελὼν τὸν στέφανον, ἢν λυπῇς τί με,
ἵνα μᾶλλον ἀλγῇς.

ΚΑ.   λῆρος· οὐ γὰρ παύσομαι
πρὶν ἂν φράσῃς μοι τίς ποτ᾽ ἐστὶν οὑτοσί·
εὔνους γὰρ ὢν σοι πυνθάνομαι πάνυ σφόδρα.   25
ΧΡ. ἀλλ᾽ οὔ σε κρύψω· τῶν ἐμῶν γὰρ οἰκετῶν
πιστότατον ἡγοῦμαί σε καὶ κλεπτίστατον.
ἐγὼ θεοσεβὴς καὶ δίκαιος ὢν ἀνὴρ
κακῶς ἔπραττον καὶ πένης ἦν. ΚΑ. οἶδά τοι.
ΧΡ. ἕτεροι δ᾽ ἐπλούτουν, ἱερόσυλοι, ῥήτορες   30
καὶ συκοφάνται καὶ πονηροί. ΚΑ. πείθομαι.
ΧΡ. ἐπερησόμενος οὖν ᾠχόμην ὡς τὸν θεὸν,
τὸν ἐμὸν μὲν αὐτοῦ τοῦ ταλαιπώρου σχεδὸν
ἤδη νομίζων ἐκτετοξεῦσθαι βίον,
τὸν δ᾽ υἱὸν, ὅσπερ ὢν μόνος μοι τυγχάνει,   35
πευσόμενος εἰ χρὴ μεταβαλόντα τοὺς τρόπους
εἶναι πανοῦργον, ἄδικον, ὑγιὲς μηδὲ ἕν,
ὡς τῷ βίῳ τοῦτ᾽ αὐτὸ νομίσας συμφέρειν.
ΚΑ. τί δῆτα Φοῖβος ἔλακεν ἐκ τῶν στεμμάτων;
ΧΡ. πεύσει. σαφῶς γὰρ ὁ θεὸς εἶπέ μοι τοδί·   40
ὅτῳ ξυναντήσαιμι πρῶτον ἐξιὼν,
ἐκέλευσε τούτου μὴ μεθίεσθαί μ᾽ ἔτι,
πείθειν δ᾽ ἐμαυτῷ ξυνακολουθεῖν οἴκαδε.
ΚΑ. καὶ τῷ ξυναντᾷς δῆτα πρώτῳ; ΧΡ. τουτῳί.
ΚΑ. εἶτ᾽ οὐ ξυνίης τὴν ἐπίνοιαν τοῦ θεοῦ,   45
φράζουσαν ὦ σκαιότατέ σοι σαφέστατα
ἀσκεῖν τὸν υἱὸν τὸν ἐπιχώριον τρόπον;
ΧΡ. τῷ τοῦτο κρίνεις;
ΚΑ.   δῆλον ὁτιὴ καὶ τυφλῷ
γνῶναι δοκεῖ τοῦθ᾽, ὡς σφόδρ᾽ ἐστὶ συμφέρον
τὸ μηδὲν ἀσκεῖν ὑγιὲς ἐν τῷ νῦν χρόνῳ.   50
ΧΡ. οὐκ ἔσθ᾽ ὅπως ὁ χρησμὸς εἰς τοῦτο ῥέπει,
ἀλλ᾽ εἰς ἕτερόν τι μεῖζον. ἢν δ᾽ ἡμῖν φράσῃ

ὅστις ποτ' ἐστὶν οὑτοσὶ καὶ τοῦ χάριν
καὶ τοῦ δεόμενος ἦλθε μετὰ νῷν ἐνθαδὶ,
πυθοίμεθ' ἂν τὸν χρησμὸν ἡμῶν ὅ τι νοεῖ. 55
ΚΑ. ἄγε δὴ, σὺ πρότερον σαυτὸν ὅστις εἶ φράσον,
ἢ τἀπὶ τούτοις δρῶ. λέγειν χρὴ ταχὺ πάνυ.
ΠΛ. ἐγὼ μὲν οἰμώζειν λέγω σοι.
ΚΑ.   μανθάνεις
ὅς φησιν εἶναι;
ΧΡ.   σοὶ λέγει τοῦτ', οὐκ ἐμοί.
σκαιῶς γὰρ αὐτοῦ καὶ χαλεπῶς ἐκπυνθάνει. 60
ἀλλ' εἴ τι χαίρεις ἀνδρὸς εὐόρκου τρόποις,
ἐμοὶ φράσον. ΠΛ. κλάειν ἔγωγέ σοι λέγω.
ΚΑ. δέχου τὸν ἄνδρα καὶ τὸν ὄρνιν τοῦ θεοῦ.
ΧΡ. οὔ τοι μὰ τὴν Δήμητρα χαιρήσεις ἔτι.
ΚΑ. εἰ μὴ φράσεις γὰρ, ἀπό σ' ὀλῶ κακὸν κακῶς. 65
ΠΛ. ὦ τᾶν, ἀπαλλάχθητον ἀπ' ἐμοῦ. ΧΡ. πώμαλα.
ΚΑ. καὶ μὴν ὃ λέγω βέλτιστόν ἐστ', ὦ δέσποτα·
ἀπολῶ τὸν ἄνθρωπον κάκιστα τουτονί.
ἀναθεὶς γὰρ ἐπὶ κρημνόν τιν' αὐτὸν καταλιπὼν
ἄπειμ', ἵν' ἐκεῖθεν ἐκτραχηλισθῇ πεσών. 70
ΧΡ. ἀλλ' αἶρε ταχέως. ΠΛ. μηδαμῶς.
ΧΡ.   οὔκουν ἐρεῖς;
ΠΛ. ἀλλ' ἢν πύθησθέ μ' ὅστις εἴμ', εὖ οἶδ' ὅτι
κακόν τί μ' ἐργάσεσθε κοὐκ ἀφήσετον.
ΧΡ. νὴ τοὺς θεοὺς ἡμεῖς γ', ἐὰν βούλῃ γε σύ.
ΠΛ. μέθεσθέ νύν μου πρῶτον. ΧΡ. ἤν, μεθίεμεν. 75
ΠΛ. ἀκούετον δή. δεῖ γὰρ ὡς ἔοικέ με
λέγειν ἃ κρύπτειν ἦ παρεσκευασμένος.
ἐγὼ γάρ εἰμι Πλοῦτος.
ΧΡ.   ὦ μιαρώτατε
ἀνδρῶν ἁπάντων, εἶτ' ἐσίγας Πλοῦτος ὤν;

ΚΑ. σὺ Πλοῦτος, οὕτως ἀθλίως διακείμενος;   80

ΧΡ. ὦ Φοῖβ' Ἄπολλον καὶ θεοὶ καὶ δαίμονες
καὶ Ζεῦ, τί φῄς; ἐκεῖνος ὄντως εἶ σύ; ΠΛ. ναί.

ΧΡ. ἐκεῖνος αὐτός; ΠΛ. αὐτότατος.

ΧΡ.   πόθεν οὖν, φράσον,
αὐχμῶν βαδίζεις;

ΠΛ.   ἐκ Πατροκλέους ἔρχομαι,
ὃς οὐκ ἐλούσατ' ἐξ ὅτουπερ ἐγένετο.   85

ΧΡ. τουτὶ δὲ τὸ κακὸν πῶς ἔπαθες; κάτειπέ μοι.

ΠΛ. ὁ Ζεύς με ταῦτ' ἔδρασεν ἀνθρώποις φθονῶν.
ἐγὼ γὰρ ὢν μειράκιον ἠπείλησ' ὅτι
ὡς τοὺς δικαίους καὶ σοφοὺς καὶ κοσμίους
μόνους βαδιοίμην· ὁ δέ μ' ἐποίησεν τυφλόν,   90
ἵνα μὴ διαγιγνώσκοιμι τούτων μηδένα.
οὕτως ἐκεῖνος τοῖσι χρηστοῖσι φθονεῖ.

ΧΡ. καὶ μὴν διὰ τοὺς χρηστούς γε τιμᾶται μόνους
καὶ τοὺς δικαίους. ΠΛ. ὁμολογῶ σοι.

ΧΡ.   φέρε, τί οὖν;
εἰ πάλιν ἀναβλέψειας ὥσπερ καὶ πρὸ τοῦ,   95
φεύγοις ἂν ἤδη τοὺς πονηρούς; ΠΛ. φήμ' ἐγώ.

ΧΡ. ὡς τοὺς δικαίους δ' ἂν βαδίζοις;

ΠΛ.   πάνυ μὲν οὖν·
πολλοῦ γὰρ αὐτοὺς οὐχ ἑόρακα διὰ χρόνου.

ΧΡ. καὶ θαῦμά γ' οὐδέν· οὐδ' ἐγὼ γὰρ ὁ βλέπων.

ΠΛ. ἄφετόν με νῦν. ἴστον γὰρ ἤδη τἀπ' ἐμοῦ.   100

ΧΡ. μὰ Δί', ἀλλὰ πολλῷ μᾶλλον ἑξόμεσθά σου.

ΠΛ. οὐκ ἠγόρευον ὅτι παρέξειν πράγματα
ἐμέλλετόν μοι;

ΧΡ.   καὶ σύ γ', ἀντιβολῶ, πιθοῦ,
καὶ μή μ' ἀπολίπῃς· οὐ γὰρ εὑρήσεις ἐμοῦ
ζητῶν ἔτ' ἄνδρα τοὺς τρόπους βελτίονα·   105

μὰ τὸν Δί'· οὐ γὰρ ἔστιν ἄλλος πλὴν ἐγώ.

ΠΛ. ταυτὶ λέγουσι πάντες· ἡνίκ' ἂν δέ μου
τύχωσ' ἀληθῶς καὶ γένωνται πλούσιοι,
ἀτεχνῶς ὑπερβάλλουσι τῇ μοχθηρίᾳ.

ΧΡ. ἔχει μὲν οὕτως, εἰσὶ δ' οὐ πάντες κακοί.   110

ΠΛ. μὰ Δί', ἀλλ' ἀπαξάπαντες.   ΚΑ. οἰμώξει μακρά.

ΧΡ. σοὶ δ' ὡς ἂν εἰδῇς ὅσα, παρ' ἡμῖν ἢν μένῃς,
γενήσετ' ἀγαθά, πρόσεχε τὸν νοῦν, ἵνα πύθῃ.
οἶμαι γάρ, οἶμαι, σὺν θεῷ δ' εἰρήσεται,
ταύτης ἀπαλλάξειν σε τῆς ὀφθαλμίας,   115
βλέψαι ποιήσας.

ΠΛ.   μηδαμῶς τοῦτ' ἐργάσῃ.
οὐ βούλομαι γὰρ πάλιν ἀναβλέψαι.   ΧΡ. τί φής ;

ΚΑ. ἄνθρωπος οὗτός ἐστιν ἄθλιος φύσει.

ΠΛ. ὁ Ζεὺς μὲν οὖν οἶδ' ὡς τὰ τούτων μῶρ' ἔμ' εἰ
πύθοιτ' ἂν ἐπιτρίψειε.   120

ΧΡ.   νῦν δ' οὐ τοῦτο δρᾷ,
ὅστις σε προσπταίοντα περινοστεῖν ἐᾷ ;

ΠΛ. οὐκ οἶδ'· ἐγὼ δ' ἐκεῖνον ὀρρωδῶ πάνυ.

ΧΡ. ἄληθες, ὦ δειλότατε πάντων δαιμόνων ;
οἴει γὰρ εἶναι τὴν Διὸς τυραννίδα
καὶ τοὺς κεραυνοὺς ἀξίους τριωβόλου,   125
ἐὰν ἀναβλέψῃς σὺ κἂν μικρὸν χρόνον ;

ΠΛ. ἆ, μὴ λέγ', ὦ πονηρέ, ταῦτ'.

ΧΡ.   ἔχ' ἥσυχος.
ἐγὼ γὰρ ἀποδείξω σὲ τοῦ Διὸς πολὺ
μεῖζον δυνάμενον.   ΠΛ. ἐμὲ σύ ;

ΧΡ.   νὴ τὸν οὐρανόν.
αὐτίκα γὰρ ἄρχει διὰ τίν' ὁ Ζεὺς τῶν θεῶν ;   130

ΚΑ. διὰ τἀργύριον· πλεῖστον γάρ ἐστ' αὐτῷ.

ΧΡ.   φέρε,

τίς οὖν ὁ παρέχων ἐστὶν αὐτῷ τοῦθ'; ΚΑ. ὁδί.

ΧΡ. θύουσι δ' αὐτῷ διὰ τίν'; οὐ διὰ τουτονί;

ΚΑ. καὶ νὴ Δί' εὔχονταί γε πλουτεῖν ἄντικρυς.

ΧΡ. οὔκουν ὅδ' ἐστὶν αἴτιος, καὶ ῥᾳδίως   135
παύσει' ἂν, εἰ βούλοιτο, ταῦθ'; ΠΛ. ὁτιὴ τί δή;

ΧΡ. ὅτι οὐδ' ἂν εἷς θύσειεν ἀνθρώπων ἔτι,
οὐ βοῦν ἂν, οὐχὶ ψαιστὸν, οὐκ ἄλλ' οὐδεὲν,
μὴ βουλομένου σοῦ. ΠΛ. πῶς;

ΧΡ.   ὅπως; οὐκ ἔσθ' ὅπως
ὠνήσεται δήπουθεν, ἢν σὺ μὴ παρὼν   140
αὐτὸς διδῷς τἀργύριον, ὥστε τοῦ Διὸς
τὴν δύναμιν, ἢν λυπῇ τι, καταλύσεις μόνος.

ΠΛ. τί λέγεις; δι' ἐμὲ θύουσιν αὐτῷ;

ΧΡ.   φήμ' ἐγώ.
καὶ νὴ Δί' εἴ τί γ' ἔστι λαμπρὸν καὶ καλὸν
ἢ χάριεν ἀνθρώποισι, διὰ σὲ γίγνεται.   145
ἅπαντα τῷ πλουτεῖν γάρ ἐσθ' ὑπήκοα.

ΚΑ. ἔγωγέ τοι διὰ μικρὸν ἀργυρίδιον
δοῦλος γεγένημαι, διὰ τὸ μὴ πλουτεῖν ἴσως.

ΧΡ. τέχναι δὲ πᾶσαι διὰ σὲ καὶ σοφίσματα   160
ἐν τοῖσιν ἀνθρώποισίν ἐσθ' εὑρημένα.
ὁ μὲν γὰρ αὐτῶν σκυτοτομεῖ καθήμενος,
ἕτερος δὲ χαλκεύει τις, ὁ δὲ τεκταίνεται.
ὁ δὲ χρυσοχοεῖ γε, χρυσίον παρὰ σοῦ λαβὼν,
ὁ δὲ λωποδυτεῖ γε νὴ Δί', ὁ δὲ τοιχωρυχεῖ,   165
ὁ δὲ γναφεύει γ', ὁ δέ γε πλύνει κώδια,
ὁ δὲ βυρσοδεψεῖ γ', ὁ δέ γε πωλεῖ κρόμμυα.

ΠΛ. οἴμοι τάλας, ταυτί μ' ἐλάνθανεν πάλαι.

ΚΑ. μέγας δὲ βασιλεὺς οὐχὶ διὰ τοῦτον κομᾷ;   170
ἐκκλησία δ' οὐχὶ διὰ τοῦτον γίγνεται;

ΧΡ. τί δέ; τὰς τριήρεις οὐ σὺ πληροῖς; εἰπέ μοι.

ΚΑ. τὸ δ' ἐν Κορίνθῳ ξενικὸν οὐχ οὗτος τρέφει;
ὁ Πάμφιλος δ' οὐχὶ διὰ τοῦτον κλαύσεται ;
ὁ βελονοπώλης δ' οὐχὶ μετὰ τοῦ Παμφίλου ; 175
ΧΡ. Φιλέψιος δ' οὐχ ἕνεκα σοῦ μύθους λέγει ;
ἡ ξυμμαχία δ' οὐ διὰ σὲ τοῖς Αἰγυπτίοις ;
ἐρᾷ δὲ Λαΐς οὐ διὰ σὲ Φιλωνίδου ;
ΚΑ. ὁ Τιμοθέου δὲ πύργος 180
ΧΡ. ἐμπέσοι γέ σοι.
τὰ δὲ πράγματ' οὐχὶ διὰ σὲ πάντα πράττεται ;
μονώτατος γὰρ εἶ σὺ πάντων αἴτιος,
καὶ τῶν κακῶν καὶ τῶν ἀγαθῶν, εὖ ἴσθ' ὅτι.
ΚΑ. κρατοῦσι γοῦν κἂν τοῖς πολέμοις ἑκάστοτε
ἐφ' οἷς ἂν οὗτος ἐπικαθέζηται μόνον. 185
ΠΛ. ἐγὼ τοσαῦτα δυνατός εἰμ' εἷς ὢν ποιεῖν ;
ΧΡ. καὶ ναὶ μὰ Δία τούτων γε πολλῷ πλείονα·
ὥστ' οὐδὲ μεστὸς σοῦ γέγον' οὐδεὶς πώποτε.
τῶν μὲν γὰρ ἄλλων ἐστὶ πάντων πλησμονή·
ἔρωτος ΚΑ. ἄρτων ΧΡ. μουσικῆς ΚΑ. τραγημάτων
ΧΡ. τιμῆς ΚΑ. πλακούντων 191
ΧΡ. ἀνδραγαθίας ΚΑ. ἰσχάδων
ΧΡ. φιλοτιμίας ΚΑ. μάζης ΧΡ. στρατηγίας
ΚΑ. φακῆς.
ΧΡ. σοῦ δ' ἐγένετ' οὐδεὶς μεστὸς οὐδεπώποτε.
ἀλλ' ἢν τάλαντά τις λάβῃ τριακαίδεκα,
πολὺ μᾶλλον ἐπιθυμεῖ λαβεῖν ἑκκαίδεκα· 195
κἂν ταῦτ' ἀνύσηται, τετταράκοντα βούλεται,
ἤ φησιν οὐ βιωτὸν αὑτῷ τὸν βίον.
ΠΛ. εὖ τοι λέγειν ἔμοιγε φαίνεσθον πάνυ·
πλὴν ἓν μόνον δέδοικα.
ΧΡ. φράζε τοῦ πέρι.
ΠΛ. ὅπως ἐγὼ τὴν δύναμιν ἣν ὑμεῖς φατὲ 200

ἔχειν με, ταύτης δεσπότης γενήσομαι.
ΧΡ. νὴ τὸν Δί᾽· ἀλλὰ καὶ λέγουσι πάντες ὡς
δειλότατόν ἐσθ᾽ ὁ πλοῦτος.
ΠΛ.   ἥκιστ᾽, ἀλλά με
τοιχωρύχος τις διέβαλ᾽. ἐσδὺς γάρ ποτε
οὐκ εἶχεν ἐς τὴν οἰκίαν οὐδὲν λαβεῖν,   205
εὑρὼν ἀπαξάπαντα κατακεκλειμένα·
εἶτ᾽ ὠνόμασέ μου τὴν πρόνοιαν δειλίαν.
ΧΡ. μή νυν μελέτω σοι μηδέν· ὡς, ἐὰν γένῃ
ἀνὴρ πρόθυμος αὐτὸς ἐς τὰ πράγματα,
βλέποντ᾽ ἀποδείξω σ᾽ ὀξύτερον τοῦ Λυγκέως.   210
ΠΛ. πῶς οὖν δυνήσει τοῦτο δρᾶσαι θνητὸς ὤν;
ΧΡ. ἔχω τιν᾽ ἀγαθὴν ἐλπίδ᾽ ἐξ ὧν εἶπέ μοι
ὁ Φοῖβος αὐτὸς Πυθικὴν σείσας δάφνην.
ΠΛ. κἀκεῖνος οὖν σύνοιδε ταῦτα; ΧΡ. φήμ᾽ ἐγώ.
ΠΛ. ὁρᾶτε.   215
ΧΡ.   μὴ φρόντιζε μηδέν, ὦγαθέ.
ἐγὼ γάρ, εὖ τοῦτ᾽ ἴσθι, κἂν δῇ μ᾽ ἀποθανεῖν,
αὐτὸς διαπράξω ταῦτα. ΚΑ. κἂν βούλῃ γ᾽, ἐγώ.
ΧΡ. πολλοὶ δ᾽ ἔσονται χἄτεροι νῷν ξύμμαχοι,
ὅσοις δικαίοις οὖσιν οὐκ ἦν ἄλφιτα.
ΠΛ. παπαῖ, πονηρούς γ᾽ εἶπας ἡμῖν συμμάχους.   220
ΧΡ. οὐκ, ἤν γε πλουτήσωσιν ἐξ ἀρχῆς πάλιν.
ἀλλ᾽ ἴθι σὺ μὲν ταχέως δραμὼν ΚΑ. τί δρῶ; λέγε.
ΧΡ. τοὺς ξυγγεώργους κάλεσον, εὑρήσεις δ᾽ ἴσως
ἐν τοῖς ἀγροῖς αὐτοὺς ταλαιπωρουμένους,
ὅπως ἂν ἴσον ἕκαστος ἐνταυθὶ παρὼν   225
ἡμῖν μετάσχῃ τοῦδε τοῦ Πλούτου μέρος.
ΚΑ. καὶ δὴ βαδίζω· τουτοδὶ κρεάδιον
τῶν ἔνδοθέν τις εἰσενεγκάτω λαβών.
ΧΡ. ἐμοὶ μελήσει τοῦτό γ᾽· ἀλλ᾽ ἀνύσας τρέχε.

ΠΛΟΥΤΟΣ.   11

σὺ δ', ὦ κράτιστε Πλοῦτε πάντων δαιμόνων,   230
εἴσω μετ' ἐμοῦ δεῦρ' εἴσιθ'· ἡ γὰρ οἰκία
αὕτη 'στὶν ἣν δεῖ χρημάτων σε τήμερον
μεστὴν ποιῆσαι καὶ δικαίως κἀδίκως.
ΠΛ. ἀλλ' ἄχθομαι μὲν εἰσιὼν νὴ τοὺς θεοὺς
εἰς οἰκίαν ἑκάστοτ' ἀλλοτρίαν πάνυ·   235
ἀγαθὸν γὰρ ἀπέλαυσ' οὐδὲν αὐτοῦ πώποτε.
ἢν μὲν γὰρ ὡς φειδωλὸν εἰσελθὼν τύχω,
εὐθὺς κατώρυξέν με κατὰ τῆς γῆς κάτω·
κἄν τις προσέλθῃ χρηστὸς ἄνθρωπος φίλος
αἰτῶν λαβεῖν τι μικρὸν ἀργυρίδιον,   240
ἔξαρνός ἐστι μηδ' ἰδεῖν με πώποτε.
ἢν δ' ὡς παραπλῆγ' ἄνθρωπον εἰσελθὼν τύχω,
πόρναισι καὶ κύβοισι παραβεβλημένος
γυμνὸς θύραζ' ἐξέπεσον ἐν ἀκαρεῖ χρόνῳ.
ΧΡ. μετρίου γὰρ ἀνδρὸς οὐκ ἐπέτυχες πώποτε.   245
ἐγὼ δὲ τούτου τοῦ τρόπου πώς εἰμ' ἀεί.
χαίρω τε γὰρ φειδόμενος ὡς οὐδεὶς ἀνὴρ
πάλιν τ' ἀναλῶν, ἡνίκ' ἂν τούτου δέῃ.
ἀλλ' εἰσίωμεν, ὡς ἰδεῖν σε βούλομαι
καὶ τὴν γυναῖκα καὶ τὸν υἱὸν τὸν μόνον,   250
ὃν ἐγὼ φιλῶ μάλιστα μετά σέ. ΠΛ. πείθομαι.
ΧΡ. τί γὰρ ἄν τις οὐχὶ πρὸς σὲ τἀληθῆ λέγοι;
ΚΑ. ὦ πολλὰ δὴ τῷ δεσπότῃ ταυτὸν θυμὸν φαγόντες,
ἄνδρες φίλοι καὶ δημόται καὶ τοῦ πονεῖν ἐρασταί,
ἴτ' ἐγκονεῖτε, σπεύδεθ', ὡς ὁ καιρὸς οὐχὶ μέλλειν,
ἀλλ' ἔστ' ἐπ' αὐτῆς τῆς ἀκμῆς, ᾗ δεῖ παρόντ'
ἀμύνειν.   256
ΧΟ. οὔκουν ὁρᾷς ὁρμωμένους ἡμᾶς πάλαι προθύμως,
ὡς εἰκός ἐστιν ἀσθενεῖς γέροντας ἄνδρας ἤδη;
σὺ δ' ἀξιοῖς ἴσως με θεῖν, πρὶν ταῦτα καὶ φράσαι μοι

ὅτου χάριν μ' ὁ δεσπότης ὁ σὸς κέκληκε δεῦρο. 260
ΚΑ. οὔκουν πάλαι δήπου λέγω; σὺ δ' αὐτὸς οὐκ ἀκούεις.
ὁ δεσπότης γάρ φησιν ὑμᾶς ἡδέως ἅπαντας
ψυχροῦ βίου καὶ δυσκόλου ζήσειν ἀπαλλαγέντας.
ΧΟ. ἔστιν δὲ δὴ τί καὶ πόθεν τὸ πρᾶγμα τοῦθ' ὅ φησιν;
ΚΑ. ἔχων ἀφῖκται δεῦρο πρεσβύτην τιν', ὦ πονηροὶ, 265
ῥυπῶντα, κυφὸν, ἄθλιον, ῥυσὸν, μαδῶντα, νωδόν.
ΧΟ. ὦ χρυσὸν ἀγγείλας ἐπῶν, πῶς φῇς; πάλιν φράσον
μοι.
δηλοῖς γὰρ αὐτὸν σωρὸν ἥκειν χρημάτων ἔχοντα.
ΚΑ. πρεσβυτικῶν μὲν οὖν κακῶν ἔγωγ' ἔχοντα σωρόν.
ΧΟ. μῶν ἀξιοῖς φενακίσας ἡμᾶς ἀπαλλαγῆναι 271
ἀζήμιος, καὶ ταῦτ' ἐμοῦ βακτηρίαν ἔχοντος;
ΚΑ. πάντως γὰρ ἄνθρωπὸν φύσει τοιοῦτον εἰς τὰ πάντα
ἡγεῖσθέ μ' εἶναι κοὐδὲν ἂν νομίζεθ' ὑγιὲς εἰπεῖν;
ΧΟ. ὡς σεμνὸς οὑπίτριπτος· αἱ κνῆμαι δέ σου βοῶσιν
ἰοὺ ἰού, τὰς χοίνικας καὶ τὰς πέδας ποθοῦσαι. 276
ΚΑ. ἐν τῇ σορῷ νυνὶ λαχὸν τὸ γράμμα σου δικάζειν,
σὺ δ' οὐ βαδίζεις; ὁ δὲ Χάρων τὸ ξύμβολον δί-
δωσιν.
ΧΟ. διαρραγείης. ὡς μόθων εἶ καὶ φύσει κόβαλος, 279
ὅστις φενακίζεις, φράσαι δ' οὔπω τέτληκας ἡμῖν
ὅτου χάριν μ' ὁ δεσπότης ὁ σὸς κέκληκε δεῦρο·
οἳ πολλὰ μοχθήσαντες, οὐκ οὔσης σχολῆς, προθύμως
δεῦρ' ἤλθομεν, πολλῶν θύμων ῥίζας διεκπερῶντες.
ΚΑ. ἀλλ' οὐκέτ' ἂν κρύψαιμι. τὸν Πλοῦτον γὰρ, ὦνδρες, ἥκει
ἄγων ὁ δεσπότης, ὃς ὑμᾶς πλουσίους ποιήσει; 285
ΧΟ. ὄντως γὰρ ἔστι πλουσίοις ἡμῖν ἅπασιν εἶναι;
ΚΑ. νὴ τοὺς θεοὺς, Μίδας μὲν οὖν, ἢν ὦτ' ὄνου λάβητε.

ΧΟ. ὡς ἥδομαι καὶ τέρπομαι καὶ βούλομαι χορεῦσαι
ὑφ' ἡδονῆς, εἴπερ λέγεις ὄντως σὺ ταῦτ' ἀληθῆ.

ΚΑ. καὶ μὴν ἐγὼ βουλήσομαι θρεττανελὸ τὸν Κύκλωπα
μιμούμενος καὶ τοῖν ποδοῖν ὡδὶ παρενσαλεύων   291
ὑμᾶς ἄγειν. ἀλλ' εἷα τέκεα θαμίν' ἐπαναβοῶντες
βληχώμενοί τε προβατίων
αἰγῶν τε κιναβρώντων μέλη,
ἕπεσθε ποιμαίνοντί μοι· τράγοι δ' ἀκρατιεῖσθε.   295

ΧΟ. ἡμεῖς δέ γ' αὖ ζητήσομεν θρεττανελὸ τὸν Κύκλωπα
βληχώμενοι, σὲ τουτονὶ πινῶντα καταλαβόντες,
πήραν ἔχοντα λάχανά τ' ἄγρια δροσερά, κραι-
   παλῶντα,
ἡγούμενον τοῖς προβατίοις,
εἰκῇ δὲ καταδαρθόντα που,   300
μέγαν λαβόντες ἡμμένον σφηκίσκον ἐκτυφλῶσαι.

ΚΑ. ἀλλ' εἷα νῦν τῶν σκωμμάτων ἀπαλλαγέντες ἤδη
ὑμεῖς ἐπ' ἄλλ' εἶδος τρέπεσθ',
ἐγὼ δ' ἰὼν ἤδη λάθρα
βουλήσομαι τοῦ δεσπότου
λαβών τιν' ἄρτον καὶ κρέας   320
μασώμενος τὸ λοιπὸν οὕτω τῷ κόπῳ ξυνεῖναι.

ΧΡ. χαίρειν μὲν ὑμᾶς ἐστιν, ὦνδρες δημόται,
ἀρχαῖον ἤδη προσαγορεύειν καὶ σαπρόν·
ἀσπάζομαι δ', ὁτιὴ προθύμως ἥκετε
καὶ συντεταμένως κοὐ κατεβλακευμένως.   325
ὅπως δέ μοι καὶ τἄλλα συμπαραστάται
ἔσεσθε καὶ σωτῆρες ὄντως τοῦ θεοῦ.

ΧΟ. θάρρει· βλέπειν γὰρ ἄντικρυς δόξεις μ' Ἄρη.
δεινὸν γάρ, εἰ τριωβόλου μὲν οὕνεκα
ὠστιζόμεσθ' ἑκάστοτ' ἐν τἠκκλησίᾳ,   330
αὐτὸν δὲ τὸν Πλοῦτον παρείην τῳ λαβεῖν.

ΧΡ. καὶ μὴν ὁρῶ καὶ Βλεψίδημον τουτονὶ
προσιόντα· δῆλος δ' ἐστὶν ὅτι τοῦ πράγματος
ἀκήκοέν τι τῇ βαδίσει καὶ τῷ τάχει.

ΒΛ. τί ἂν οὖν τὸ πρᾶγμ' εἴη ; πόθεν καὶ τίνι τρόπῳ   335
Χρεμύλος πεπλούτηκ' ἐξαπίνης ; οὐ πείθομαι.
καίτοι λόγος γ' ἦν νὴ τὸν Ἡρακλέα πολὺς
ἐπὶ τοῖσι κουρείοισι τῶν καθημένων,
ὡς ἐξαπίνης ἀνὴρ γεγένηται πλούσιος.
ἔστιν δέ μοι τοῦτ' αὐτὸ θαυμάσιον, ὅπως   340
χρηστόν τι πράττων τοὺς φίλους μεταπέμπεται.
οὔκουν ἐπιχώριόν γε πρᾶγμ' ἐργάζεται.

ΧΡ. ἀλλ' οὐδὲν ἀποκρύψας ἐρῶ νὴ τοὺς θεούς.
ὦ Βλεψίδημ', ἄμεινον ἢ χθὲς πράττομεν,
ὥστε μετέχειν ἔξεστιν· εἶ γὰρ τῶν φίλων.   345

ΒΛ. γέγονας δ' ἀληθῶς, ὡς λέγουσι, πλούσιος ;

ΧΡ. ἔσομαι μὲν οὖν αὐτίκα μάλ', ἢν θεὸς θέλῃ.
ἔνι γάρ τις, ἔνι κίνδυνος ἐν τῷ πράγματι.

ΒΛ. ποῖός τις ;   ΧΡ. οἷος

ΒΛ.   λέγ' ἀνύσας ὅ τι φῂς ποτε.

ΧΡ. ἢν μὲν κατορθώσωμεν, εὖ πράττειν ἀεί·   350
ἢν δὲ σφαλῶμεν, ἐπιτετρίφθαι τὸ παράπαν.

ΒΛ. τουτὶ πονηρὸν φαίνεται τὸ φορτίον,
καί μ' οὐκ ἀρέσκει. τό τε γὰρ ἐξαίφνης ἄγαν
οὕτως ὑπερπλουτεῖν τό τ' αὖ δεδοικέναι
πρὸς ἀνδρὸς οὐδὲν ὑγιές ἐστ' εἰργασμένου.   355

ΧΡ. πῶς οὐδὲν ὑγιές ;

ΒΛ.   εἴ τι κεκλοφὼς νὴ Δία
ἐκεῖθεν ἥκεις ἀργύριον ἢ χρυσίον
παρὰ τοῦ θεοῦ, κἄπειτ' ἴσως σοι μεταμέλει.

ΧΡ. Ἄπολλον ἀποτρόπαιε, μὰ Δί' ἐγὼ μὲν οὔ.

ΒΛ. παῦσαι φλυαρῶν, ὠγάθ'· οἶδα γὰρ σαφῶς.   360

ΧΡ. σὺ μηδὲν εἰς ἔμ᾽ ὑπονόει τοιουτονί.

ΒΛ. φεῦ·
ὡς οὐδὲν ἀτεχνῶς ὑγιές ἐστιν οὐδενός,
ἀλλ᾽ εἰσὶ τοῦ κέρδους ἅπαντες ἥττονες.

ΧΡ. οὔ τοι μὰ τὴν Δήμητρ᾽ ὑγιαίνειν μοι δοκεῖς.

ΒΛ. ὡς πολὺ μεθέστηχ᾽ ὧν πρότερον εἶχεν τρόπων. 365

ΧΡ. μελαγχολᾷς, ὦνθρωπε, νὴ τὸν οὐρανόν.

ΒΛ. ἀλλ᾽ οὐδὲ τὸ βλέμμ᾽ αὐτὸ κατὰ χώραν ἔχει,
ἀλλ᾽ ἐστὶν ἐπίδηλόν τι πεπανουργηκότι.

ΧΡ. σὺ μὲν οἶδ᾽ ὃ κρώζεις· ὡς ἐμοῦ τι κεκλοφότος
ζητεῖς μεταλαβεῖν. ΒΛ. μεταλαβεῖν ζητῶ; τίνος;

ΧΡ. τὸ δ᾽ ἐστὶν οὐ τοιοῦτον, ἀλλ᾽ ἑτέρως ἔχον. 371

ΒΛ. μῶν οὐ κέκλοφας, ἀλλ᾽ ἥρπακας; ΧΡ. κακοδαιμονᾷς.

ΒΛ. ἀλλ᾽ οὐδὲ μὴν ἀπεστέρηκάς γ᾽ οὐδένα;

ΧΡ. οὐ δῆτ᾽ ἔγωγ᾽.

ΒΛ.   ὦ Ἡράκλεις, φέρε, ποῖ τις ἂν
τράποιτο; τἀληθὲς γὰρ οὐκ ἐθέλεις φράσαι. 375

ΧΡ. κατηγορεῖς γὰρ πρὶν μαθεῖν τὸ πρᾶγμά μου.

ΒΛ. ὦ τᾶν, ἐγώ τοι τοῦτ᾽ ἀπὸ σμικροῦ πάνυ
ἐθέλω διαπρᾶξαι πρὶν πυθέσθαι τὴν πόλιν,
τὸ στόμ᾽ ἐπιβύσας κέρμασιν τῶν ῥητόρων.

ΧΡ. καὶ μὴν φίλως γ᾽ ἄν μοι δοκεῖς νὴ τοὺς θεοὺς 380
τρεῖς μνᾶς ἀναλώσας λογίσασθαι δώδεκα.

ΒΛ. ὁρῶ τιν᾽ ἐπὶ τοῦ βήματος καθεδούμενον,
ἱκετηρίαν ἔχοντα μετὰ τῶν παιδίων
καὶ τῆς γυναικὸς, κοὐ διοίσοντ᾽ ἄντικρυς
τῶν Ἡρακλειδῶν οὐδ᾽ ὁτιοῦν τῶν Παμφίλου. 385

ΧΡ. οὐκ, ὦ κακόδαιμον, ἀλλὰ τοὺς χρηστοὺς μόνους
ἔγωγε καὶ τοὺς δεξιοὺς καὶ σώφρονας
ἀπαρτὶ πλουτῆσαι ποιήσω.

ΒΛ.   τί σὺ λέγεις;

οὕτω πάνυ πολλὰ κέκλοφας;

ΧΡ.   οἴμοι τῶν κακῶν,

ἀπολεῖς ΒΛ. σὺ μὲν οὖν σεαυτὸν, ὥς γ' ἐμοὶ δοκεῖς.

ΧΡ. οὐ δῆτ', ἐπεὶ τὸν Πλοῦτον, ὦ μοχθηρὲ σὺ,   391

ἔχω. ΒΛ. σὺ Πλοῦτον; ποῖον; ΧΡ. αὐτὸν τὸν θεόν.

ΒΛ. καὶ ποῦ 'στιν; ΧΡ. ἔνδον. ΒΛ. ποῦ;

ΧΡ.   παρ' ἐμοί. ΒΛ. παρὰ σοί; ΧΡ. πάνυ.

ΒΛ. οὐκ ἐς κόρακας; Πλοῦτος παρὰ σοί;

ΧΡ.   νὴ τοὺς θεούς.

ΒΛ. λέγεις ἀληθῆ; ΧΡ. φημί. ΒΛ. πρὸς τῆς Ἑστίας;

ΧΡ. νὴ τὸν Ποσειδῶ. ΒΛ. τὸν θαλάττιον λέγεις; 396

ΧΡ. εἰ δ' ἔστιν ἕτερός τις Ποσειδῶν, τὸν ἕτερον.

ΒΛ. εἶτ' οὐ διαπέμπεις καὶ πρὸς ἡμᾶς τοὺς φίλους;

ΧΡ. οὐκ ἔστι πω τὰ πράγματ' ἐν τούτῳ.

ΒΛ.   τί φῄς;

οὐ τῷ μεταδοῦναι;   400

ΧΡ.   μὰ Δία. δεῖ γὰρ πρῶτα ΒΛ. τί;

ΧΡ. βλέψαι ποιῆσαι νὼ ΒΛ. τίνα βλέψαι; φράσον.

ΧΡ. τὸν Πλοῦτον ὥσπερ πρότερον ἑνί γέ τῳ τρόπῳ.

ΒΛ. τυφλὸς γὰρ ὄντως ἐστί; ΧΡ. νὴ τὸν οὐρανόν.

ΒΛ. οὐκ ἐτὸς ἄρ' ὡς ἔμ' ἦλθεν οὐδεπώποτε.

ΧΡ. ἀλλ' ἢν θεοὶ θέλωσι, νῦν ἀφίξεται.   405

ΒΛ. οὔκουν ἰατρὸν εἰσαγαγεῖν ἐχρῆν τινά;

ΧΡ. τίς δῆτ' ἰατρός ἐστι νῦν ἐν τῇ πόλει;

οὔτε γὰρ ὁ μισθὸς οὐδὲν ἔστ' οὔθ' ἡ τέχνη.

ΒΛ. σκοπῶμεν. ΧΡ. ἀλλ' οὐκ ἔστιν. ΒΛ. οὐδ' ἐμοὶ
δοκεῖ.

ΧΡ. μὰ Δί', ἀλλ' ὅπερ πάλαι παρεσκευαζόμην   410

ἐγὼ, κατακλίνειν αὐτὸν εἰς Ἀσκληπιοῦ

κράτιστόν ἐστι.

ΒΛ.   πολὺ μὲν οὖν νὴ τοὺς θεούς.

μή νυν διάτριβ', ἀλλ' ἄννε πράττων ἕν γέ τι.
ΧΡ. καὶ μὴν βαδίζω.   ΒΛ. σπεῦδέ νυν.
ΧΡ.   τοῦτ' αὐτὸ δρῶ.
ΠΕ. ὦ θερμὸν ἔργον κἀνόσιον καὶ παράνομον   415
τολμῶντε δρᾶν ἀνθρωπαρίω κακοδαίμονε,
ποῖ ποῖ; τί φεύγετ'; οὐ μενεῖτον; ΒΛ. Ἡράκλεις.
ΠΕ. ἐγὼ γὰρ ὑμᾶς ἐξολῶ κακοὺς κακῶς·
τόλμημα γὰρ τολμᾶτον οὐκ ἀνασχετὸν,
ἀλλ' οἷον οὐδεὶς ἄλλος οὐδεπώποτε   420
οὔτε θεὸς οὔτ' ἄνθρωπος· ὥστ' ἀπολώλατον.
ΧΡ. σὺ δ' εἶ τίς; ὠχρὰ μὲν γὰρ εἶναί μοι δοκεῖς.
ΒΛ. ἴσως Ἐρινύς ἐστιν ἐκ τραγῳδίας·
βλέπει γέ τοι μανικόν τι καὶ τραγῳδικόν.
ΧΡ. ἀλλ' οὐκ ἔχει γὰρ δᾷδας.   ΒΛ. οὐκοῦν κλαύσεται.
ΠΕ. οἴεσθε δ' εἶναι τίνα με;   426
ΧΡ.   πανδοκεύτριαν,
ἢ λεκιθόπωλιν.   οὐ γὰρ ἂν τοσουτονὶ
ἐνέκραγες ἡμῖν οὐδὲν ἠδικημένη.
ΠΕ. ἄληθες; οὐ γὰρ δεινότατα δεδράκατον,
ζητοῦντες ἐκ πάσης με χώρας ἐκβαλεῖν;   430
ΧΡ. οὔκουν ὑπόλοιπον τὸ βάραθρόν σοι γίγνεται;
ἀλλ' ἥτις εἶ λέγειν σ' ἐχρῆν αὐτίκα μάλα.
ΠΕ. ἦ σφὼ ποιήσω τήμερον δοῦναι δίκην
ἀνθ' ὧν ἐμὲ ζητεῖτον ἐνθένδ' ἀφανίσαι.
ΒΛ. ἆρ' ἐστὶν ἡ καπηλὶς ἡκ τῶν γειτόνων,   435
ἢ ταῖς κοτύλαις ἀεί με διαλυμαίνεται;
ΠΕ. Πενία μὲν οὖν, ἢ σφῷν ξυνοικῶ πόλλ' ἔτη.
ΒΛ. ἄναξ Ἄπολλον καὶ θεοί, ποῖ τις φύγῃ;
ΧΡ. οὗτος, τί δρᾷς; ὦ δειλότατον σὺ θηρίον,
οὐ παραμενεῖς; ΒΛ. ἥκιστα πάντων.   440
ΧΡ.   οὐ μενεῖς;

ἀλλ' ἄνδρε δύο γυναῖκα φεύγομεν μίαν;

ΒΛ. Πενία γάρ ἐστιν, ὦ πονήρ', ἧς οὐδαμοῦ
οὐδὲν πέφυκε ζῷον ἐξωλέστερον.

ΧΡ. στῆθ', ἀντιβολῶ σε, στῆθι.

ΒΛ.   μὰ Δί' ἐγὼ μὲν οὔ.

ΧΡ. καὶ μὴν λέγω, δεινότατον ἔργον παρὰ πολὺ   445
ἔργων ἁπάντων ἐργασόμεθ', εἰ τὸν θεὸν
ἔρημον ἀπολιπόντε ποι φευξούμεθα
τηνδὶ δεδιότε, μηδὲ διαμαχούμεθα.

ΒΛ. ποίοις ὅπλοισιν ἢ δυνάμει πεποιθότες;
ποῖον γὰρ οὐ θώρακα, ποίαν δ' ἀσπίδα   450
οὐκ ἐνέχυρον τίθησιν ἡ μιαρωτάτη;

ΧΡ. θάρρει· μόνος γὰρ ὁ θεὸς οὗτος οἶδ' ὅτι
τροπαῖον ἂν στήσαιτο τῶν ταύτης τρόπων.

ΠΕ. γρύζειν δὲ καὶ τολμᾶτον, ὦ καθάρματε,
ἐπ' αὐτοφώρῳ δεινὰ δρῶντ' εἰλημμένω;   455

ΧΡ. σὺ δ', ὦ κάκιστ' ἀπολουμένη, τί λοιδορεῖ
ἡμῖν προσελθοῦσ' οὐδ' ὁτιοῦν ἀδικουμένη;

ΠΕ. οὐδὲν γάρ, ὦ πρὸς τῶν θεῶν, νομίζετε
ἀδικεῖν με τὸν Πλοῦτον ποιεῖν πειρωμένω
βλέψαι πάλιν;   460

ΧΡ.   τί οὖν ἀδικοῦμεν τοῦτό σε,
εἰ πᾶσιν ἀνθρώποισιν ἐκπορίζομεν
ἀγαθόν; ΠΕ. τί δ' ἂν ὑμεῖς ἀγαθὸν ἐξεύροιθ':

ΧΡ.   ὅ τι;
σὲ πρῶτον ἐκβαλόντες ἐκ τῆς Ἑλλάδος.

ΠΕ. ἔμ' ἐκβαλόντες; καὶ τί ἂν νομίζετον
κακὸν ἐργάσασθαι μεῖζον ἀνθρώπους;   465

ΧΡ.   ὅ τι;
εἰ τοῦτο δρᾶν μέλλοντες ἐπιλαθοίμεθα.

ΠΕ. καὶ μὴν περὶ τούτου σφῷν ἐθέλω δοῦναι λόγον

τὸ πρῶτον αὐτοῦ· κἂν μὲν ἀποφήνω μόνην
ἀγαθῶν ἁπάντων οὖσαν αἰτίαν ἐμὲ
ὑμῖν δι' ἐμέ τε ζῶντας ὑμᾶς· εἰ δὲ μὴ,   470
ποιεῖτον ἤδη τοῦθ' ὅ τι ἂν ὑμῖν δοκῇ.

ΧΡ. ταυτὶ σὺ τολμᾷς, ὦ μιαρωτάτη, λέγειν;

ΠΕ. καὶ σύ γε διδάσκου· πάνυ γὰρ οἶμαι ῥᾳδίως
ἅπανθ' ἁμαρτάνοντά σ' ἀποδείξειν ἐγώ,
εἰ τοὺς δικαίους φῇς ποιήσειν πλουσίους.   475

ΧΡ. ὦ τύμπανα καὶ κύφωνες οὐκ ἀρήξετε;

ΠΕ. οὐ δεῖ σχετλιάζειν καὶ βοᾶν πρὶν ἂν μάθῃς.

ΧΡ. καὶ τίς δύναιτ' ἂν μὴ βοᾶν ἰοὺ ἰοὺ
τοιαῦτ' ἀκούων; ΠΕ. ὅστις ἐστὶν εὖ φρονῶν.

ΧΡ. τί δῆτά σοι τίμημ' ἐπιγράψω τῇ δίκῃ,   480
ἐὰν ἁλῷς; ΠΕ. ὅ τι σοι δοκεῖ.

ΧΡ.   καλῶς λέγεις.

ΠΕ. τὸ γὰρ αὔτ', ἐὰν ἡττᾶσθε, καὶ σφὼ δεῖ παθεῖν.

ΧΡ. ἱκανοὺς νομίζεις δῆτα θανάτους εἴκοσιν;

ΒΛ. ταύτῃ γε· νῷν δὲ δύ' ἀποχρήσουσιν μόνω.

ΠΕ. οὐκ ἂν φθάνοιτε τοῦτο πράττοντες· τί γὰρ   485
ἔχοι τις ἂν δίκαιον ἀντειπεῖν ἔτι;

ΧΟ. ἀλλ' ἤδη χρῆν τι λέγειν ὑμᾶς σοφὸν ᾧ νικήσετε τηνδὶ
ἐν τοῖσι λόγοις ἀντιλέγοντες, μαλακὸν δ' ἐνδώ-
σετε μηδέν.

ΧΡ. φανερὸν μὲν ἔγωγ' οἶμαι γνῶναι τοῦτ' εἶναι πᾶσιν
ὁμοίως,
ὅτι τοὺς χρηστοὺς τῶν ἀνθρώπων εὖ πράττειν
ἐστὶ δίκαιον,   490
τοὺς δὲ πονηροὺς καὶ τοὺς ἀθέους τούτων τἀναντία
δήπου.
τοῦτ' οὖν ἡμεῖς ἐπιθυμοῦντες μόλις εὕρομεν ὥστε
γενέσθαι

2—2

βούλευμα καλὸν καὶ γενναῖον καὶ χρήσιμον εἰς
ἅπαν ἔργον.
ἢν γὰρ ὁ Πλοῦτος νυνὶ βλέψῃ καὶ μὴ τυφλὸς
ὢν περινοστῇ,
ὡς τοὺς ἀγαθοὺς τῶν ἀνθρώπων βαδιεῖται κοὐκ
ἀπολείψει,   495
τοὺς δὲ πονηροὺς καὶ τοὺς ἀθέους φευξεῖται· κᾆτα
ποιήσει
πάντας χρηστοὺς καὶ πλουτοῦντας δήπου τά τε
θεῖα σέβοντας.
καίτοι τούτου τοῖς ἀνθρώποις τίς ἂν ἐξεύροι ποτ᾽
ἄμεινον ;
ΒΛ. οὗτις· ἐγώ σοι τούτου μάρτυς· μηδὲν ταύτην γ᾽
ἀνερώτα.
ΧΡ. ὡς μὲν γὰρ νῦν ἡμῖν ὁ βίος τοῖς ἀνθρώποις διά-
κειται,   500
τίς ἂν οὐχ ἡγοῖτ᾽ εἶναι μανίαν, κακοδαιμονίαν τ᾽
ἔτι μᾶλλον ;
πολλοὶ μὲν γὰρ τῶν ἀνθρώπων ὄντες πλουτοῦσι
πονηροὶ,
ἀδίκως αὐτὰ ξυλλεξάμενοι· πολλοὶ δ᾽ ὄντες πάνυ
χρηστοὶ
πράττουσι κακῶς καὶ πεινῶσιν μετὰ σοῦ τε τὰ
πλεῖστα σύνεισιν.
οὐκοῦν εἶναί φημ᾽, εἰ παύσει ταύτην βλέψας ποθ᾽
ὁ Πλοῦτος,   505
ὁδὸν ἥν τις ἰὼν τοῖς ἀνθρώποις ἀγάθ᾽ ἂν μείζω
πορίσειεν.
ΠΕ. ἀλλ᾽ ὦ πάντων ῥᾷστ᾽ ἀνθρώπων ἀναπεισθέντ᾽ οὐχ
ὑγιαίνειν
δύο πρεσβύτα, ξυνθιασῶτα τοῦ ληρεῖν καὶ παρα-
παίειν,

εἰ τοῦτο γένοιθ᾽ ὃ ποθεῖθ᾽ ὑμεῖς, οὔ φημ᾽ ἂν
λυσιτελεῖν σφῷν.
εἰ γὰρ ὁ Πλοῦτος βλέψειε πάλιν διανείμειέν τ᾽
ἴσον αὐτὸν,   510
οὔτε τέχνην ἂν τῶν ἀνθρώπων οὔτ᾽ ἂν σοφίαν
μελετῴη
οὐδείς· ἀμφοῖν δ᾽ ἱμῖν τούτοιν ἀφανισθέντοιν ἐθελήσει
τίς χαλκεύειν ἢ ναυπηγεῖν ἢ ῥάπτειν ἢ τροχο-
ποιεῖν
ἢ σκυτοτομεῖν ἢ πλινθουργεῖν ἢ πλύνειν ἢ σκυ-
λοδεψεῖν
ἢ γῆς ἀρότροις ῥήξας δάπεδον καρπὸν Δηοῦς
θερίσασθαι,   515
ἢν ἐξῇ ζῆν ἀργοῖς ὑμῖν τούτων πάντων ἀμελοῦσιν;
ΧΡ. λῆρον ληρεῖς. ταῦτα γὰρ ἡμῖν πάνθ᾽ ὅσα νῦν δὴ
κατέλεξας
οἱ θεράποντες μοχθήσουσιν.
ΠΕ.   πόθεν οὖν ἕξεις θεράποντας;
ΧΡ. ὠνησόμεθ᾽ ἀργυρίου δήπου.
ΠΕ.   τίς δ᾽ ἔσται πρῶτον ὁ πωλῶν,
ὅταν ἀργύριον κἀκεῖνος ἔχῃ;   520
ΧΡ.   κερδαίνειν βουλόμενός τις
ἔμπορος ἥκων ἐκ Θετταλίας παρὰ πλείστων ἀν-
δραποδιστῶν.
ΠΕ. ἀλλ᾽ οὐδ᾽ ἔσται πρῶτον ἁπάντων οὐδεὶς οὐδ᾽ ἀνδραποδιστὴς
κατὰ τὸν λόγον ὃν σὺ λέγεις δήπου. τίς γὰρ
πλουτῶν ἐθελήσει
κινδυνεύων περὶ τῆς ψυχῆς τῆς αὐτοῦ τοῦτο
ποιῆσαι;

ὥστ᾽ αὐτὸς ἀροῦν ἐπαναγκασθεὶς καὶ σκάπτειν
τἄλλα τε μοχθεῖν 525
ὀδυνηρότερον τρίψεις βίοτον πολὺ τοῦ νῦν.

ΧΡ. ἐς κεφαλὴν σοί.

ΠΕ. ἔτι δ᾽ οὐχ ἕξεις οὔτ᾽ ἐν κλίνῃ καταδαρθεῖν· οὐ
γὰρ ἔσονται·
οὔτ᾽ ἐν δάπισιν· τίς γὰρ ὑφαίνειν ἐθελήσει χρυσίου ὄντος;
οὔτε μύροισιν μυρίσαι στακτοῖς, ὁπόταν νύμφην
ἀγάγησθον·
οὔθ᾽ ἱματίων βαπτῶν δαπάναις κοσμῆσαι ποικιλομόρφων. 530
καίτοι τί πλέον πλουτεῖν ἐστιν πάντων τούτων
ἀποροῦντα;
παρ᾽ ἐμοῦ δ᾽ ἔστιν ταῦτ᾽ εὔπορα πάνθ᾽ ὑμῖν ὧν
δεῖσθον· ἐγὼ γὰρ
τὸν χειροτέχνην ὥσπερ δέσποιν᾽ ἐπαναγκάζουσα
κάθημαι
διὰ τὴν χρείαν καὶ τὴν πενίαν ζητεῖν ὁπόθεν βίον ἕξει.

ΧΡ. σὺ γὰρ ἂν πορίσαι τί δύναι᾽ ἀγαθόν, πλὴν φῴδων
ἐκ βαλανείου, 535
καὶ παιδαρίων ὑποπεινώντων καὶ γραϊδίων κολοσυρτοῦ;
φθειρῶν τ᾽ ἀριθμὸν καὶ κωνώπων καὶ ψυλλῶν
οὐδὲ λέγω σοι
ὑπὸ τοῦ πλήθους, αἳ βομβοῦσαι περὶ τὴν κεφαλὴν
ἀνιῶσιν,
ἐπεγείρουσαι καὶ φράζουσαι, πεινήσεις, ἀλλ᾽ ἐπα-
νίστω.
πρὸς δέ γε τούτοις ἀνθ᾽ ἱματίου μὲν ἔχειν ῥάκος·
ἀντὶ δὲ κλίνης 540

στιβάδα σχοίνων κόρεων μεστὴν, ἢ τοὺς εὕδοντας
    ἐγείρει·
καὶ φορμὸν ἔχειν ἀντὶ τάπητος σαπρόν· ἀντὶ δὲ
    προσκεφαλαίου,
λίθον εὐμεγέθη πρὸς τῇ κεφαλῇ· σιτεῖσθαι δ' ἀντὶ
    μὲν ἄρτων
μαλάχης πτόρθους, ἀντὶ δὲ μάζης φυλλεῖ' ἰσχνῶν
    ῥαφανίδων,
ἀντὶ δὲ θράνου στάμνου κεφαλὴν κατεαγότος, ἀντὶ
    δὲ μάκτρας   545
φιδάκνης πλευρὰν ἐρρωγυῖαν καὶ ταύτην. ἆρά γε
    πολλῶν
ἀγαθῶν πᾶσιν τοῖς ἀνθρώποις ἀποφαίνω σ' αἴτιον
    οὖσαν ;
ΠΕ. σὺ μὲν οὐ τὸν ἐμὸν βίον εἴρηκας, τὸν τῶν πτωχῶν
    δ' ὑπεκρούσω.
ΧΡ. οὐκοῦν δήπου τῆς πτωχείας πενίαν φαμὲν εἶναι
    ἀδελφήν.
ΠΕ. ὑμεῖς γ' οἵπερ καὶ Θρασυβούλῳ Διονύσιον εἶναι
    ὅμοιον.   550
ἀλλ' οὐχ οὑμὸς τοῦτο πέπονθεν βίος οὐ μὰ Δί',
    οὐδέ γε μέλλει.
πτωχοῦ μὲν γὰρ βίος, ὃν σὺ λέγεις, ζῆν ἐστιν
    μηδὲν ἔχοντα·
τοῦ δὲ πένητος ζῆν φειδόμενον καὶ τοῖς ἔργοις
    προσέχοντα,
περιγίγνεσθαι δ' αὐτῷ μηδέν, μὴ μέντοι μηδ' ἐπι-
    λείπειν.
ΧΡ. ὡς μακαρίτην, ὦ Δάματερ, τὸν βίον αὐτοῦ κατέ-
    λεξας,   555

εἰ φεισάμενος καὶ μοχθήσας καταλείψει μηδὲ
   ταφῆναι.

ΠΕ. σκώπτειν πειρᾷ καὶ κωμῳδεῖν τοῦ σπουδάζειν
   ἀμελήσας,
οὐ γιγνώσκων ὅτι τοῦ Πλούτου παρέχω βελτίονας
   ἄνδρας
καὶ τὴν γνώμην καὶ τὴν ἰδέαν. παρὰ τῷ μὲν γὰρ
   ποδαγρῶντες
καὶ γαστρώδεις καὶ παχύκνημοι καὶ πίονές εἰσιν
   ἀσελγῶς,   560
παρ᾽ ἐμοὶ δ᾽ ἰσχνοὶ καὶ σφηκώδεις καὶ τοῖς ἐχθροῖς
   ἀνιαροί.

ΧΡ. ἀπὸ τοῦ λιμοῦ γὰρ ἴσως αὐτοῖς τὸ σφηκῶδες σὺ
   πορίζεις.

ΠΕ. περὶ σωφροσύνης ἤδη τοίνυν περανῶ σφῷν κἀνα-
   διδάξω
ὅτι κοσμιότης οἰκεῖ μετ᾽ ἐμοῦ, τοῦ Πλούτου δ᾽
   ἐστὶν ὑβρίζειν.

ΧΡ. πάνυ γοῦν κλέπτειν κόσμιόν ἐστιν καὶ τοὺς τοί-
   χους διορύττειν.   565

[ΒΛ. νὴ τὸν Δί᾽, εἰ δεῖ λαθεῖν αὐτόν, πῶς οὐχὶ κόσμιόν
   ἐστιν;]

ΠΕ. σκέψαι τοίνυν ἐν ταῖς πόλεσιν τοὺς ῥήτορας, ὡς
   ὁπόταν μὲν
ὦσι πένητες, περὶ τὸν δῆμον καὶ τὴν πόλιν εἰσὶ
   δίκαιοι,
πλουτήσαντες δ᾽ ἀπὸ τῶν κοινῶν παραχρῆμ᾽ ἄδικοι
   γεγένηνται,
ἐπιβουλεύουσί τε τῷ πλήθει καὶ τῷ δήμῳ πολε-
   μοῦσιν.   570

ΧΡ. ἀλλ' οὐ ψεύδει τούτων γ' οὐδέν, καίπερ σφόδρα
βάσκανος οὖσα.
ἀτὰρ οὐχ ἧττόν γ' οὐδὲν κλαύσει, μηδὲν ταύτῃ
γε κομήσῃς,
ὁτιὴ ζητεῖς τοῦτ' ἀναπείθειν ἡμᾶς, ὡς ἔστιν
ἀμείνων
πενία πλούτου.

ΠΕ.   καὶ σύ γ' ἐλέγξαι μ' οὔπω δύνασαι
περὶ τούτου,
ἀλλὰ φλυαρεῖς καὶ πτερυγίζεις.   575

ΧΡ.   καὶ πῶς φεύγουσί σ' ἅπαντες ;

ΠΕ. ὅτι βελτίους αὐτοὺς ποιῶ. σκέψασθαι δ' ἔστι
μάλιστα
ἀπὸ τῶν παίδων· τοὺς γὰρ πατέρας φεύγουσι,
φρονοῦντας ἄριστα
αὐτοῖς. οὕτω διαγιγνώσκειν χαλεπὸν πρᾶγμ' ἐστὶ
δίκαιον.

ΧΡ. τὸν Δία φήσεις ἆρ' οὐκ ὀρθῶς διαγιγνώσκειν τὸ
κράτιστον·
κἀκεῖνος γὰρ τὸν πλοῦτον ἔχει.   580

ΒΛ.   ταύτην δ' ἡμῖν ἀποπέμπει.

ΠΕ. ἀλλ' ὦ Κρονικαῖς λήμαις ὄντως λημῶντες τὰς
φρένας ἄμφω,
ὁ Ζεὺς δήπου πένεται, καὶ τοῦτ' ἤδη φανερῶς σε
διδάξω.
εἰ γὰρ ἐπλούτει, πῶς ἂν ποιῶν τὸν Ὀλυμπικὸν
αὐτὸς ἀγῶνα,
ἵνα τοὺς Ἕλληνας ἅπαντας ἀεὶ δι' ἔτους πέμπτου
ξυναγείρει,
ἀνεκήρυττεν τῶν ἀσκητῶν τοὺς νικῶντας στεφανώσας   585

κοτίνῳ στεφάνῳ; καίτοι χρυσῷ μᾶλλον ἐχρῆν,
εἴπερ ἐπλούτει.

ΧΡ. οὐκοῦν τούτῳ δήπου δηλοῖ τιμῶν τὸν πλοῦτον
ἐκεῖνος·
φειδόμενος γὰρ καὶ βουλόμενος τούτου μηδὲν δα-
πανᾶσθαι,
λήροις ἀναδῶν τοὺς νικῶντας τὸν πλοῦτον ἐᾷ
παρ᾽ ἑαυτῷ.

ΠΕ. πολὺ τῆς πενίας πρᾶγμ᾽ αἴσχιον ζητεῖς αὐτῷ
περιάψαι,   590
εἰ πλούσιος ὢν ἀνελεύθερός ἐσθ᾽ οὑτωσὶ καὶ φιλο-
κερδής.

ΧΡ. ἀλλὰ σέ γ᾽ ὁ Ζεὺς ἐξολέσειεν κοτίνῳ στεφάνῳ
στεφανώσας.

ΠΕ. τὸ γὰρ ἀντιλέγειν τολμᾶν ὑμᾶς ὡς οὐ πάντ᾽ ἔστ᾽
ἀγάθ᾽ ὑμῖν
διὰ τὴν Πενίαν.

ΧΡ.   παρὰ τῆς Ἑκάτης ἔξεστιν τοῦτο πυθέσθαι,
εἴτε τὸ πλουτεῖν εἴτε τὸ πεινῆν βέλτιον. φησὶ
γὰρ αὕτη   595
τοὺς μὲν ἔχοντας καὶ πλουτοῦντας δεῖπνον κατὰ
μῆν᾽ ἀποπέμπειν,
τοὺς δὲ πένητας τῶν ἀνθρώπων ἁρπάζειν πρὶν
καταθεῖναι.
ἀλλὰ φθείρου καὶ μὴ γρύξῃς
ἔτι μηδ᾽ ὁτιοῦν.
οὐ γὰρ πείσεις, οὐδ᾽ ἢν πείσῃς.   600

ΠΕ. ὦ πόλις Ἄργους, κλύεθ᾽ οἷα λέγει.

ΧΡ. Παύσωνα κάλει τὸν ξύσσιτον.

ΠΕ. τί πάθω τλήμων;

ΧΡ. ἔρρ᾽ ἐς κόρακας θᾶττον ἀφ᾽ ἡμῶν.

ΠΕ. εἰμι δὲ ποῖ γῆς ;   605
ΧΡ. ἐς τὸν κύφων·· ἀλλ᾽ οὐ μέλλειν
    χρῆν σ᾽, ἀλλ᾽ ἀνύτειν.
ΠΕ. ἦ μὴν ὑμεῖς γ᾽ ἔτι μ᾽ ἐνταυθὶ
    μεταπέμψεσθον.
ΧΡ. τότε νοστήσεις· νῦν δὲ φθείρου.   610
    κρεῖττον γάρ μοι πλουτεῖν ἐστὶν,
    σὲ δ᾽ ἐᾶν κλάειν μακρὰ τὴν κεφαλήν.
ΒΛ. νὴ Δί᾽ ἔγωγ᾽ οὖν ἐθέλω πλουτῶν
    εὐωχεῖσθαι μετὰ τῶν παίδων
    τῆς τε γυναικὸς, καὶ λουσάμενος   615
    λιπαρὸς χωρῶν ἐκ βαλανείου
    τῶν χειροτεχνῶν·
    καὶ τῆς Πενίας καταπαρδεῖν.
ΧΡ. αὕτη μὲν ἡμῖν ἠπίτριπτος οἴχεται.
    ἐγὼ δὲ καὶ σύ γ᾽ ὡς τάχιστα τὸν θεὸν   620
    ἐγκατακλινοῦντ᾽ ἄγωμεν εἰς Ἀσκληπιοῦ.
ΒΛ. καὶ μὴ διατρίβωμέν γε, μὴ πάλιν τις αὖ
    ἐλθὼν διακωλύσῃ τι τῶν προὔργου ποιεῖν.
ΧΡ. παῖ Καρίων, τὰ στρώματ᾽ ἐκφέρειν σ᾽ ἐχρῆν,
    αὐτόν τ᾽ ἄγειν τὸν Πλοῦτον, ὡς νομίζεται,   625
    καὶ τἄλλ᾽ ὅσ᾽ ἐστὶν ἔνδον ηὐτρεπισμένα.
ΚΑ. ὦ πλεῖστα Θησείοις μεμυστιλημένοι
    γέροντες ἄνδρες ἐπ᾽ ὀλιγίστοις ἀλφίτοις,
    ὡς εὐτυχεῖθ᾽, ὡς μακαρίως πεπράγατε,
    ἄλλοι θ᾽ ὅσοις μέτεστι τοῦ χρηστοῦ τρόπου.   630
ΧΟ. τί δ᾽ ἔστιν ὦ βέλτιστε τῶν σαυτοῦ φίλων ;
    φαίνει γὰρ ἥκειν ἄγγελος χρηστοῦ τινος.
ΚΑ. ὁ δεσπότης πέπραγεν εὐτυχέστατα,
    μᾶλλον δ᾽ ὁ Πλοῦτος αὐτός· ἀντὶ γὰρ τυφλοῦ
    ἐξωμμάτωται καὶ λελάμπρυνται κόρας,   635

Ἀσκληπιοῦ παιῶνος εὐμενοῦς τυχών.

ΧΟ. λέγεις μοι χαρὰν, λέγεις μοι βοάν.

ΚΑ. πάρεστι χαίρειν, ἤν τε βούλησθ᾽ ἤν τε μή.

ΧΟ. ἀναβοάσομαι τὸν εὔπαιδα καὶ
μέγα βροτοῖσι φέγγος Ἀσκληπιόν.   640

ΓΥ. τίς ἡ βοή ποτ᾽ ἐστίν; ἆρ᾽ ἀγγέλλεται
χρηστόν τι; τοῦτο γὰρ ποθοῦσ᾽ ἐγὼ πάλαι
ἔνδον κάθημαι περιμένουσα τουτονί.

ΚΑ. ταχέως ταχέως φέρ᾽ οἶνον, ὦ δέσποιν᾽, ἵνα
καὐτὴ πίῃς· φιλεῖς δὲ δρῶσ᾽ αὐτὸ σφόδρα·   645
ὡς ἀγαθὰ συλλήβδην ἅπαντά σοι φέρω.

ΓΥ. καὶ ποῦ 'στιν; ΚΑ. ἐν τοῖς λεγομένοις εἴσει τάχα.

ΓΥ. πέραινε τοίνυν ὅ τι λέγεις ἀνύσας ποτέ.

ΚΑ. ἄκουε τοίνυν, ὡς ἐγὼ τὰ πράγματα
ἐκ τῶν ποδῶν ἐς τὴν κεφαλήν σοι πάντ᾽ ἐρῶ.   650

ΓΥ. μὴ δῆτ᾽ ἔμοιγ᾽ ἐς τὴν κεφαλήν.

ΚΑ.   μὴ τἀγαθὰ
ἃ νῦν γεγένηται; ΓΥ. μὴ μὲν οὖν τὰ πράγματα.

ΚΑ. ὡς γὰρ τάχιστ᾽ ἀφικόμεθα πρὸς τὸν θεὸν
ἄγοντες ἄνδρα τότε μὲν ἀθλιώτατον,
νῦν δ᾽ εἴ τιν᾽ ἄλλον μακάριον κεὐδαίμονα,   655
πρῶτον μὲν αὐτὸν ἐπὶ θάλατταν ἤγομεν,
ἔπειτ᾽ ἐλοῦμεν.

ΓΥ.   νὴ Δί᾽ εὐδαίμων ἄρ᾽ ἦν
ἀνὴρ γέρων ψυχρᾷ θαλάττῃ λούμενος.

ΚΑ. ἔπειτα πρὸς τὸ τέμενος ᾖμεν τοῦ θεοῦ.
ἐπεὶ δὲ βωμῷ πόπανα καὶ προθύματα   660
καθωσιώθη, πέλανος Ἡφαίστου φλογί,
κατεκλίναμεν τὸν Πλοῦτον, ὥσπερ εἰκὸς ἦν·
ἡμῶν δ᾽ ἕκαστος στιβάδα παρεκαττύετο.

ΓΥ. ἦσαν δέ τινες κἄλλοι δεόμενοι τοῦ θεοῦ;

ΚΑ. εἰς μέν γε Νεοκλείδης, ὅς ἐστι μὲν τυφλὸς,   665
κλέπτων δὲ τοὺς βλέποντας ὑπερηκόντικεν·
ἕτεροί τε πολλοὶ παντοδαπὰ νοσήματα
ἔχοντες· ὡς δὲ τοὺς λύχνους ἀποσβέσας
ἡμῖν παρήγγειλ᾽ ἐγκαθεύδειν τοῦ θεοῦ
ὁ πρόπολος, εἰπὼν, ἤν τις αἴσθηται ψόφου,   670
σιγᾶν, ἅπαντες κοσμίως κατεκείμεθα.
κἀγὼ καθεύδειν οὐκ ἐδυνάμην, ἀλλά με
ἀθάρης χύτρα τις ἐξέπληττε κειμένη
ὀλίγον ἄπωθεν τῆς κεφαλῆς τοῦ γρᾳδίου,
ἐφ᾽ ἣν ἐπεθύμουν δαιμονίως ἐφερπύσαι.   675
ἔπειτ᾽ ἀναβλέψας ὁρῶ τὸν ἱερέα
τοὺς φθοῖς ἀφαρπάζοντα καὶ τὰς ἰσχάδας
ἀπὸ τῆς τραπέζης τῆς ἱερᾶς. μετὰ τοῦτο δὲ
περιῆλθε τοὺς βωμοὺς ἅπαντας ἐν κύκλῳ,
εἴ που πόπανον εἴη τι καταλελειμμένον·   680
ἔπειτα ταῦθ᾽ ἥγιζεν ἐς σάκταν τινά.
κἀγὼ νομίσας πολλὴν ὁσίαν τοῦ πράγματος
ἐπὶ τὴν χύτραν τὴν τῆς ἀθάρης ἀνίσταμαι.
ΓΥ. ταλάντατ᾽ ἀνδρῶν, οὐκ ἐδεδοίκεις τὸν θεόν;
ΚΑ. νὴ τοὺς θεοὺς ἔγωγε μὴ φθάσειέ με   685
ἐπὶ τὴν χύτραν ἐλθὼν ἔχων τὰ στέμματα.
ὁ γὰρ ἱερεὺς αὐτοῦ με προὐδιδάξατο.
τὸ γρᾴδιον δ᾽ ὡς ᾐσθάνετό μου τὸν ψόφον,
τὴν χεῖρ᾽ ὑφῄρει· κᾆτα συρίξας ἐγὼ
ὀδὰξ ἐλαβόμην, ὡς παρείας ὢν ὄφις.   690
ἡ δ᾽ εὐθέως τὴν χεῖρα πάλιν ἀνέσπασε,
κατέκειτο δ᾽ αὐτὴν ἐντυλίξασ᾽ ἡσυχῇ.
κἀγὼ τότ᾽ ἤδη τῆς ἀθάρης πολλὴν ἔφλων·
ἔπειτ᾽ ἐπειδὴ μεστὸς ἦν, ἀνεπαυόμην.   695
ΓΥ. ὁ δὲ θεὸς ὑμῖν οὐ προσῄειν;

ΚΑ. οὐδέπω.
μετὰ ταῦτ᾽ ἐγὼ μὲν εὐθὺς ἐνεκαλυψάμην
δείσας, ἐκεῖνος δ᾽ ἐν κύκλῳ τὰ νοσήματα
σκοπῶν περιῄει πάντα κοσμίως πάνυ.
ἔπειτα παῖς αὐτῷ λίθινον θυείδιον   710
παρέθηκε καὶ δοίδυκα καὶ κιβώτιον.
ΓΥ. λίθινον;
ΚΑ.   μὰ Δί᾽ οὐ δῆτ᾽, οὐχὶ τό γε κιβώτιον.
ΓΥ. σὺ δὲ πῶς ἑώρας, ὦ κάκιστ᾽ ἀπολούμενε,
ὃς ἐγκεκαλύφθαι φῄς;
ΚΑ.   διὰ τοῦ τριβωνίου.
ὀπὰς γὰρ εἶχεν οὐκ ὀλίγας μὰ τὸν Δία.   715
πρῶτον δὲ πάντων τῷ Νεοκλείδῃ φάρμακον
καταπλαστὸν ἐνεχείρησε τρίβειν, ἐμβαλὼν
σκορόδων κεφαλὰς τρεῖς Τηνίων. ἔπειτ᾽ ἔφλα
ἐν τῇ θυείᾳ συμπαραμιγνύων ὀπὸν
καὶ σχῖνον· εἶτ᾽ ὄξει διέμενος Σφηττίῳ,   720
κατέπλασεν αὐτοῦ τὰ βλέφαρ᾽ ἐκστρέψας, ἵνα
ὀδυνῷτο μᾶλλον. ὁ δὲ κεκραγὼς καὶ βοῶν
ἔφευγ᾽ ἀνᾴξας· ὁ δὲ θεὸς γελάσας ἔφη·
ἐνταῦθα νῦν κάθησο καταπεπλασμένος,
ἵν᾽ ὑπομνύμενον παύσω σε τῆς ἐκκλησίας.   725
ΓΥ. ὡς φιλόπολίς τίς ἐσθ᾽ ὁ δαίμων καὶ σοφός.
ΚΑ. μετὰ τοῦτο τῷ Πλούτωνι παρεκαθέζετο,
καὶ πρῶτα μὲν δὴ τῆς κεφαλῆς ἐφήψατο,
ἔπειτα καθαρὸν ἡμιτύβιον λαβὼν
τὰ βλέφαρα περιέψησεν· ἡ Πανάκεια δὲ   730
κατεπέτασ᾽ αὐτοῦ τὴν κεφαλὴν φοινικίδι
καὶ πᾶν τὸ πρόσωπον· εἶθ᾽ ὁ θεὸς ἐπόππυσεν.
ἐξῇξάτην οὖν δύο δράκοντ᾽ ἐκ τοῦ νεὼ
ὑπερφυεῖς τὸ μέγεθος. ΓΥ. ὦ φίλοι θεοί.

ΚΑ. τούτω δ᾽ ὑπὸ τὴν φοινικίδ᾽ ὑποδύνθ᾽ ἡσυχῇ 735
τὰ βλέφαρα περιέλειχον, ὥς γ᾽ ἐμοὐδόκει·
καὶ πρίν σε κοτύλας ἐκπιεῖν οἴνου δέκα
ὁ Πλοῦτος, ὦ δέσποιν᾽, ἀνεστήκει βλέπων·
ἐγὼ δὲ τὼ χεῖρ᾽ ἀνεκρότησ᾽ ὑφ᾽ ἡδονῆς,
τὸν δεσπότην τ᾽ ἤγειρον. ὁ θεὸς δ᾽ εὐθέως 740
ἠφάνισεν αὑτὸν οἵ τ᾽ ὄφεις εἰς τὸν νεών.
οἱ δ᾽ ἐγκατακείμενοι παρ᾽ αὐτῷ πῶς δοκεῖς
τὸν Πλοῦτον ἠσπάζοντο καὶ τὴν νύχθ᾽ ὅλην
ἐγρηγόρεσαν, ἕως διέλαμψεν ἡμέρα.
ἐγὼ δ᾽ ἐπῄνουν τὸν θεὸν πάνυ σφόδρα, 745
ὅτι βλέπειν ἐποίησε τὸν Πλοῦτον ταχύ,
τὸν δὲ Νεοκλείδην μᾶλλον ἐποίησεν τυφλόν.
ΓΥ. ὅσην ἔχεις τὴν δύναμιν, ὦναξ δέσποτα.
ἀτὰρ φράσον μοι, ποῦ ᾽σθ᾽ ὁ Πλοῦτος;
ΚΑ.   ἔρχεται.
ἀλλ᾽ ἦν περὶ αὐτὸν ὄχλος ὑπερφυὴς ὅσος. 750
οἱ γὰρ δίκαιοι πρότερον ὄντες καὶ βίον
ἔχοντες ὀλίγον αὐτὸν ἠσπάζοντο καὶ
ἐδεξιοῦνθ᾽ ἅπαντες ὑπὸ τῆς ἡδονῆς·
ὅσοι δ᾽ ἐπλούτουν οὐσίαν τ᾽ εἶχον συχνὴν
οὐκ ἐκ δικαίου τὸν βίον κεκτημένοι, 755
ὀφρῦς συνῆγον ἐσκυθρώπαζόν θ᾽ ἅμα.
οἱ δ᾽ ἠκολούθουν κατόπιν ἐστεφανωμένοι,
γελῶντες, εὐφημοῦντες· ἐκτυπεῖτο δὲ
ἐμβὰς γερόντων εὐρύθμοις προβήμασιν.
ἀλλ᾽ εἶ᾽ ἁπαξάπαντες ἐξ ἑνὸς λόγου 760
ὀρχεῖσθε καὶ σκιρτᾶτε καὶ χορεύετε·
οὐδεὶς γὰρ ὑμῖν εἰσιοῦσιν ἀγγελεῖ
ὡς ἄλφιτ᾽ οὐκ ἔνεστιν ἐν τῷ θυλάκῳ.
ΓΥ. νὴ τὴν Ἑκάτην, κἀγὼ δ᾽ ἀναδῆσαι βούλομαι

εὐαγγέλιά σε κριβανωτῶν ὁρμαθῷ,   765
τοιαῦτ᾽ ἀπαγγείλαντα.

ΚΑ.   μή νυν μέλλ᾽ ἔτι
ὡς ἄνδρες ἐγγύς εἰσιν ἤδη τῶν θυρῶν.

ΓΥ. φέρε νυν ἰοῦσ᾽ εἴσω κομίσω καταχύσματα
ὥσπερ νεωνήτοισιν ὀφθαλμοῖς ἐγώ.

ΚΑ. ἐγὼ δ᾽ ἀπαντῆσαί γ᾽ ἐκείνοις βούλομαι.   770

ΠΛ. καὶ προσκυνῶ γε πρῶτα μὲν τὸν "Ηλιον,
ἔπειτα σεμνῆς Παλλάδος κλεινὸν πέδον,
χώραν τε πᾶσαν Κέκροπος, ἥ μ᾽ ἐδέξατο.
αἰσχύνομαι δὲ τὰς ἐμαυτοῦ συμφορὰς,
οἵοις ἄρ᾽ ἀνθρώποις ξυνὼν ἐλάνθανον,   775
τοὺς ἀξίους δὲ τῆς ἐμῆς ὁμιλίας
ἔφευγον, εἰδὼς οὐδέν· ὦ τλήμων ἐγώ.
ὡς οὔτ᾽ ἐκεῖν᾽ ἄρ᾽ οὔτε ταῦτ᾽ ὀρθῶς ἔδρων·
ἀλλ᾽ αὐτὰ πάντα πάλιν ἀναστρέψας ἐγὼ
δείξω τὸ λοιπὸν πᾶσιν ἀνθρώποις ὅτι   780
ἄκων ἐμαυτὸν τοῖς πονηροῖς ἐνεδίδουν.

ΧΡ. βάλλ᾽ ἐς κόρακας· ὡς χαλεπόν εἰσιν οἱ φίλοι
οἱ φαινόμενοι παραχρῆμ᾽ ὅταν πράττῃ τις εὖ.
νύττουσι γὰρ καὶ φλῶσι τἀντικνήμια,
ἐνδεικνύμενος ἕκαστος εὔνοιάν τινα.   785
ἐμὲ γὰρ τίς οὐ προσεῖπε; ποῖος οὐκ ὄχλος
περιεστεφάνωσεν ἐν ἀγορᾷ πρεσβυτικός;

ΓΥ. ὦ φίλτατ᾽ ἀνδρῶν, καὶ σὺ καὶ σὺ χαίρετε.
φέρε νυν, νόμος γάρ ἐστι, τὰ καταχύσματα
ταυτὶ καταχέω σου λαβοῦσα.   790

ΠΛ.   μηδαμῶς.
ἐμοῦ γὰρ εἰσιόντος εἰς τὴν οἰκίαν
πρώτιστα καὶ βλέψαντος οὐδὲν ἐκφέρειν
πρεπῶδές ἐστιν, ἀλλὰ μᾶλλον εἰσφέρειν.

ΓΥ. εἶτ᾽ οὐχὶ δέξει δῆτα τὰ καταχύσματα;
ΠΛ. ἔνδον γε παρὰ τὴν ἑστίαν, ὥσπερ νόμος·   795
ἔπειτα καὶ τὸν φόρτον ἐκφύγοιμεν ἄν.
οὐ γὰρ πρεπῶδές ἐστι τῷ διδασκάλῳ
ἰσχάδια καὶ τρωγάλια τοῖς θεωμένοις
προβαλόντ᾽, ἐπὶ τούτοις εἶτ᾽ ἀναγκάζειν γελᾶν.
ΓΥ. εὖ πάνυ λέγεις· ὡς Δεξίνικος οὑτοσὶ   800
ἀνίσταθ᾽ ὡς ἁρπασόμενος τὰς ἰσχάδας.
ΚΑ. ὡς ἡδὺ πράττειν, ὦνδρες, ἔστ᾽ εὐδαιμόνως,
καὶ ταῦτα μηδὲν ἐξενεγκόντ᾽ οἴκοθεν.
ἡμῖν γὰρ ἀγαθῶν σωρὸς εἰς τὴν οἰκίαν
ἐπεισπέπαικεν οὐδὲν ἠδικηκόσιν.   805
[οὕτω τὸ πλουτεῖν ἐστιν ἡδὺ πρᾶγμα δή.]
ἡ μὲν σιπύη μεστή 'στι λευκῶν ἀλφίτων,
οἱ δ᾽ ἀμφορῆς οἴνου μέλανος ἀνθοσμίου.
ἅπαντα δ᾽ ἡμῖν ἀργυρίου καὶ χρυσίου
τὰ σκευάρια πλήρη 'στὶν, ὥστε θαυμάσαι.
τὸ φρέαρ δ᾽ ἐλαίου μεστόν· αἱ δὲ λήκυθοι   810
μύρου γέμουσι, τὸ δ᾽ ὑπερῷον ἰσχάδων.
ὀξὶς δὲ πᾶσα καὶ λοπάδιον καὶ χύτρα
χαλκῆ γέγονε· τοὺς δὲ πινακίσκους τοὺς σαπροὺς
τοὺς ἰχθυηροὺς ἀργυροῦς πάρεσθ᾽ ὁρᾶν.
ὁ δ᾽ ἰπνὸς γέγον᾽ ἡμῖν ἐξαπίνης ἐλεφάντινος.   815
στατῆρσι δ᾽ οἱ θεράποντες ἀρτιάζομεν.
καὶ νῦν ὁ δεσπότης μὲν ἔνδον βουθυτεῖ
ὗν καὶ τράγον καὶ κριὸν ἐστεφανωμένος,   820
ἐμὲ δ᾽ ἐξέπεμψεν ὁ καπνός. οὐχ οἷός τε γὰρ
ἔνδον μένειν ἦν. ἔδακνε γὰρ τὰ βλέφαρά μου.
ΔΙ. ἕπου μετ᾽ ἐμοῦ παιδάριον, ἵνα πρὸς τὸν θεὸν
ἴωμεν. ΚΑ. ἔα, τίς ἔσθ᾽ ὁ προσιὼν οὑτοσί;
ΔΙ. ἀνὴρ πρότερον μὲν ἄθλιος, νῦν δ᾽ εὐτυχής.   825

G. P.   3

ΚΑ. δῆλον ὅτι τῶν χρηστῶν τις, ὡς ἔοικας, εῖ.
ΔΙ. μάλιστ'. ΚΑ. ἔπειτα τοῦ δέει;
ΔΙ.   πρὸς τὸν θεὸν
ἥκω· μεγάλων γάρ μοῦστὶν ἀγαθῶν αἴτιος.
ἐγὼ γὰρ ἱκανὴν οὐσίαν παρὰ τοῦ πατρὸς
λαβὼν ἐπήρκουν τοῖς δεομένοις τῶν φίλων,   830
εἶναι νομίζων χρήσιμον πρὸς τὸν βίον.
ΚΑ. ἦ πού σε ταχέως ἐπέλιπεν τὰ χρήματα.
ΔΙ. κομιδῆ μὲν οὖν.
ΚΑ.   οὐκοῦν μετὰ ταῦτ' ἦσθ' ἄθλιος.
ΔΙ. κομιδῆ μὲν οὖν. κἀγὼ μὲν ᾤμην οὓς τέως
εὐηργέτησα δεομένους ἕξειν φίλους   835
ὄντως βεβαίους, εἰ δεηθείην ποτέ·
οἱ δ' ἐξετρέποντο κοὐκ ἐδόκουν ὁρᾶν μ' ἔτι.
ΚΑ. καὶ κατεγέλων δ', εὖ οἶδ' ὅτι.
ΔΙ.   κομιδῆ μὲν οὖν.
ΚΑ. αὐχμὸς γὰρ ὢν τῶν σκευαρίων σ' ἀπώλεσεν.
ΔΙ. ἀλλ' οὐχὶ νῦν. ἀνθ' ὧν ἐγὼ πρὸς τὸν θεὸν   840
προσευξόμενος ἥκω δικαίως ἐνθάδε.
ΚΑ. τὸ τριβώνιον δὲ τί δύναται πρὸς τῶν θεῶν,
ὃ φέρει μετὰ σοῦ τὸ παιδάριον τουτί; φράσον.
ΔΙ. καὶ τοῦτ' ἀναθήσων ἔρχομαι πρὸς τὸν θεόν.
ΚΑ. μῶν ἐνεμυήθης δῆτ' ἐν αὐτῷ τὰ μεγάλα;   845
ΔΙ. οὐκ, ἀλλ' ἐνερρίγωσ' ἔτη τριακαίδεκα.
ΚΑ. τὰ δ' ἐμβάδια; ΔΙ. καὶ ταῦτα συνεχειμάζετο.
ΚΑ. καὶ ταῦτ' ἀναθήσων ἔφερες οὖν; ΔΙ. νὴ τὸν Δία.
ΚΑ. χαρίεντά γ' ἥκεις δῶρα τῷ θεῷ φέρων.
ΣΤ. οἴμοι κακοδαίμων, ὡς ἀπόλωλα δείλαιος,   850
καὶ τρὶς κακοδαίμων καὶ τετράκις καὶ πεντάκις
καὶ δωδεκάκις καὶ μυριάκις· ἰοῦ ἰοῦ.
οὕτω πολυφόρῳ συγκέκραμαι δαίμονι.

ΚΑ. Ἄπολλον ἀποτρόπαιε καὶ θεοὶ φίλοι,
    τί ποτ' ἐστὶν ὅ τι πέπονθεν ἄνθρωπος κακόν;   855
ΣΤ. οὐ γὰρ σχέτλια πέπονθα νυνὶ πράγματα,
    ἀπολωλεκὼς ἅπαντα τἀκ τῆς οἰκίας
    διὰ τὸν θεὸν τοῦτον, τὸν ἐσόμενον τυφλὸν
    πάλιν αὖθις, ἤνπερ μὴ 'λλίπωσιν αἱ δίκαι;
ΚΑ. ἐγὼ σχεδὸν τὸ πρᾶγμα γιγνώσκειν δοκῶ.   860
    προσέρχεται γάρ τις κακῶς πράττων ἀνήρ,
    ἔοικε δ' εἶναι τοῦ πονηροῦ κόμματος.
ΔΙ. νὴ Δία, καλῶς τοίνυν ποιῶν ἀπόλλυται.
ΣΤ. ποῦ ποῦ 'σθ' ὁ μόνος ἅπαντας ἡμᾶς πλουσίους
    ὑποσχόμενος οὗτος ποιήσειν εὐθέως,   865
    εἰ πάλιν ἀναβλέψειεν ἐξ ἀρχῆς; ὁ δὲ
    πολὺ μᾶλλον ἐνίους ἐστὶν ἐξολωλεκώς.
ΚΑ. καὶ τίνα δέδρακε δῆτα τοῦτ'; ΣΤ. ἐμὲ τουτονί;
ΔΙ. ἦ τῶν πονηρῶν ἦσθα καὶ τοιχωρύχων;
ΣΤ. μὰ Δί', οὐ μὲν οὖν ἔσθ' ὑγιὲς ὑμῶν οὐδενός,   870
    κοὐκ ἔσθ' ὅπως οὐκ ἔχετέ μου τὰ χρήματα.
ΚΑ. ὡς σοβαρός, ὦ Δάματερ, εἰσελήλυθεν
    ὁ συκοφάντης. ΔΙ. δῆλον ὅτι βουλιμιᾷ.
ΣΤ. σὺ μὲν εἰς ἀγορὰν ἰὼν ταχέως οὐκ ἂν φθάνοις;
    ἐπὶ τοῦ τροχοῦ γὰρ δεῖ σ' ἐκεῖ στρεβλούμενον   875
    εἰπεῖν ἃ πεπανούργηκας. ΚΑ. οἰμώξἄρα σύ.
ΔΙ. νὴ τὸν Δία τὸν σωτῆρα, πολλοῦ γ' ἄξιος
    ἅπασι τοῖς Ἕλλησιν ὁ θεὸς οὗτος, εἰ
    τοὺς συκοφάντας ἐξολεῖ κακοὺς κακῶς.
ΣΤ. οἴμοι τάλας· μῶν καὶ σὺ μετέχων καταγελᾷς;   880
    ἐπεὶ πόθεν θοἰμάτιον εἴληφας τοδί;
    ἐχθὲς δ' ἔχοντ' εἶδόν σ' ἐγὼ τριβώνιον.
ΔΙ. οὐδὲν προτιμῶ σου. φορῶ γὰρ πριάμενος
    τὸν δακτύλιον τονδὶ παρ' Εὐδήμου δραχμῆς.

ΚΑ. ἀλλ' οὐκ ἔνεστι συκοφάντου δήγματος. 885

ΣΤ. ἆρ' οὐχ ὕβρις ταῦτ' ἐστὶ πολλή; σκώπτετον,
ὅ τι δὲ ποιεῖτον ἐνθάδ' οὐκ εἰρήκατον.
οὐκ ἐπ' ἀγαθῷ γὰρ ἐνθάδ' ἐστὸν οὐδενί.

ΚΑ. μὰ τὸν Δί' οὔκουν τῷ γε σῷ, σάφ' ἴσθ' ὅτι.

ΣΤ. ἀπὸ τῶν ἐμῶν γὰρ ναὶ μὰ Δία δειπνήσετον. 890

ΚΑ. ὡς δὴ 'π' ἀληθείᾳ σὺ μετὰ τοῦ μάρτυρος
διαρραγείης, μηδενός γ' ἐμπλήμενος.

ΣΤ. ἀρνεῖσθον; ἔνδον ἐστὶν, ὦ μιαρωτάτω,
πολὺ χρῆμα τεμαχῶν καὶ κρεῶν ὠπτημένων.
ὒ ὒ ὒ ὒ ὒ ὒ ὒ ὒ ὒ ὒ ὒ ὒ. 895

ΚΑ. κακόδαιμον, ὀσφραίνει τι;

ΔΙ.   τοῦ ψύχους γ' ἴσως,
ἐπεὶ τοιοῦτόν γ' ἀμπέχεται τριβώνιον.

ΣΤ. ταῦτ' οὖν ἀνασχέτ' ἐστὶν, ὦ Ζεῦ καὶ θεοὶ,
τούτους ὑβρίζειν εἰς ἔμ'; οἴμ' ὡς ἄχθομαι
ὅτι χρηστὸς ὢν καὶ φιλόπολις πάσχω κακῶς. 900

ΔΙ. σὺ φιλόπολις καὶ χρηστός; ΣΤ. ὡς οὐδείς γ' ἀνήρ.

ΔΙ. καὶ μὴν ἐπερωτηθεὶς ἀπόκριναί μοι, ΣΤ. τὸ τί;

ΔΙ. γεωργὸς εἶ; ΣΤ. μελαγχολᾶν μ' οὕτως οἴει;

ΔΙ. ἀλλ' ἔμπορος; ΣΤ. ναὶ, σκήπτομαί γ', ὅταν τύχω.

ΔΙ. τί δαί; τέχνην τιν' ἔμαθες; ΣΤ. οὐ μὰ τὸν Δία.

ΔΙ. πῶς οὖν διέζης ἢ πόθεν μηδὲν ποιῶν; 906

ΣΤ. τῶν τῆς πόλεώς εἰμ' ἐπιμελητὴς πραγμάτων
καὶ τῶν ἰδίων πάντων. ΔΙ. σύ; τί μαθών;

ΣΤ.   βούλομαι.

ΔΙ. πῶς οὖν ἂν εἴης χρηστὸς, ὦ τοιχωρύχε,
εἰ σοὶ προσῆκον μηδὲν εἶτ' ἀπεχθάνει; 910

ΣΤ. οὐ γὰρ προσήκει τὴν ἐμαυτοῦ μοι πόλιν
εὐεργετεῖν, ὦ κέπφε, καθ' ὅσον ἂν σθένω;

ΔΙ. εὐεργετεῖν οὖν ἐστι τὸ πολυπραγμονεῖν;

ΣΤ. τὸ μὲν οὖν βοηθεῖν τοῖς νόμοις τοῖς κειμένοις
    καὶ μὴ 'πιτρέπειν ἐάν τις ἐξαμαρτάνῃ.   915
ΔΙ. οὔκουν δικαστὰς ἐξεπίτηδες ἡ πόλις
    ἄρχειν καθίστησιν; ΣΤ. κατηγορεῖ δὲ τίς;
ΔΙ. ὁ βουλόμενος.
ΣΤ.   οὔκουν ἐκεῖνός εἰμ' ἐγώ.
    ὥστ' εἰς ἔμ' ἥκει τῆς πόλεως τὰ πράγματα.
ΔΙ. νὴ Δία, πονηρόν τἄρα προστάτην ἔχει.   920
    ἐκεῖνο δ' οὐ βούλοι' ἂν, ἡσυχίαν ἔχων
    ζῆν ἀργός;
ΣΤ.   ἀλλὰ προβατίου βίον λέγεις
    εἰ μὴ φανεῖται διατριβή τις τῷ βίῳ.
ΔΙ. οὐδ' ἂν μεταμάθοις;
ΣΤ.   οὐδ' ἂν εἰ δοίης γέ μοι
    τὸν Πλοῦτον αὐτὸν καὶ τὸ Βάττου σίλφιον.   925
ΔΙ. κατάθου ταχέως θοἰμάτιον. ΚΑ. οὗτος, σοὶ λέγει.
ΔΙ. ἔπειθ' ὑπόλυσαι. ΚΑ. πάντα ταῦτα σοὶ λέγει.
ΣΤ. καὶ μὴν προσελθέτω πρὸς ἔμ' ὑμῶν ἐνθαδὶ
    ὁ βουλόμενος. ΚΑ. οὔκουν ἐκεῖνός εἰμ' ἐγώ.
ΣΤ. οἴμοι τάλας, ἀποδύομαι μεθ' ἡμέραν.   930
ΚΑ. σὺ γὰρ ἀξιοῖς τἀλλότρια πράττων ἐσθίειν.
ΣΤ. ὁρᾷς ἃ ποιεῖ; ταῦτ' ἐγὼ μαρτύρομαι.
ΚΑ. ἀλλ' οἴχεται φεύγων ὃν ἦγες μάρτυρα.
ΣΤ. οἴμοι περιείλημμαι μόνος. ΚΑ. νυνὶ βοᾷς;
ΣΤ. οἴμοι μάλ' αὖθις.   935
ΚΑ.   δὸς σύ μοι τὸ τριβώνιον,
    ἵν' ἀμφιέσω τὸν συκοφάντην τουτονί.
ΔΙ. μὴ δῆθ'· ἱερὸν γάρ ἐστι τοῦ Πλούτου πάλαι.
ΚΑ. ἔπειτα ποῦ κάλλιον ἀνατεθήσεται
    ἢ περὶ πονηρὸν ἄνδρα καὶ τοιχωρύχον;
    Πλοῦτον δὲ κοσμεῖν ἱματίοις σεμνοῖς πρέπει.   940

ΔΙ. τοῖς δ' ἐμβαδίοις τί χρήσεταί τις; εἰπέ μοι.

ΚΑ. καὶ ταῦτα πρὸς τὸ μέτωπον αὐτίκα δὴ μάλα
ὥσπερ κοτίνῳ προσπατταλεύσω τουτῳί.

ΣΥ. ἄπειμι· γιγνώσκω γὰρ ἥττων ὢν πολὺ
ὑμῶν· ἐὰν δὲ σύζυγον λάβω τινὰ   945
καὶ σύκινον, τοῦτον τὸν ἰσχυρὸν θεὸν
ἐγὼ ποιήσω τήμερον δοῦναι δίκην,
ὁτιὴ καταλύει περιφανῶς εἷς ὢν μόνος
τὴν δημοκρατίαν, οὔτε τὴν βουλὴν πιθὼν
τὴν τῶν πολιτῶν οὔτε τὴν ἐκκλησίαν.   950

ΔΙ. καὶ μὴν ἐπειδὴ τὴν πανοπλίαν τὴν ἐμὴν
ἔχων βαδίζεις, ἐς τὸ βαλανεῖον τρέχε·
ἔπειτ' ἐκεῖ κορυφαῖος ἑστηκὼς θέρου.
κἀγὼ γὰρ εἶχον τὴν στάσιν ταύτην ποτέ.

ΚΑ. ἀλλ' ὁ βαλανεὺς ἕλξει θύραζ' αὐτὸν λαβών.   955
νὼ δ' εἰσίωμεν, ἵνα προσεύξῃ τὸν θεόν.

ΓΡ. ἆρ', ὦ φίλοι γέροντες, ἐπὶ τὴν οἰκίαν
ἀφίγμεθ' ὄντως τοῦ νέου τούτου θεοῦ,   960
ἢ τῆς ὁδοῦ τὸ παράπαν ἡμαρτήκαμεν;

ΧΟ. ἀλλ' ἴσθ' ἐπ' αὐτὰς τὰς θύρας ἀφιγμένη,
ὦ μειρακίσκη· πυνθάνει γὰρ ὡρικῶς.

ΓΡ. φέρε νῦν ἐγὼ τῶν ἔνδοθεν καλέσω τινά.

ΧΡ. μὴ δῆτ'· ἐγὼ γὰρ αὐτὸς ἐξελήλυθα.   965
ἀλλ' ὅ τι μάλιστ' ἐλήλυθας λέγειν σ' ἐχρῆν.

ΓΡ. πέπονθα δεινὰ καὶ παράνομ' ὦ φίλτατε·
ἀφ' οὗ γὰρ ὁ θεὸς οὗτος ἤρξατο βλέπειν,
ἀβίωτον εἶναί μοι πεποίηκε τὸν βίον.

ΧΡ. τί δ' ἔστιν; ἦ που καὶ σὺ συκοφάντρια   970
ἐν ταῖς γυναιξὶν ἦσθα; ΓΡ. μὰ Δί' ἐγὼ μὲν οὔ.

ΧΡ. ἀλλ' οὐ λαχοῦσ' ἔπινες ἐν τῷ γράμματι;

ΓΡ. σκώπτεις· ἐγὼ δὲ κατακέκνισμαι δειλάκρα.

ΧΡ. οὔκουν ἐρεῖς ἀνύσασα τὸν κνισμὸν τίνα;

ΓΡ. ἄκουέ νυν. ἦν μοί τι μειράκιον φίλον,   975
πενιχρὸν μὲν, ἄλλως δ᾽ εὐπρόσωπον καὶ καλὸν
καὶ χρηστόν· εἰ γάρ του δεηθείην ἐγώ,
ἅπαντ᾽ ἐποίει κοσμίως μοι καὶ καλῶς·
ἐγὼ δ᾽ ἐκείνῳ ταῦτα πάνθ᾽ ὑπηρέτουν.

ΧΡ. τί δ᾽ ἦν ὅ τι σου μάλιστ᾽ ἐδεῖθ᾽ ἑκάστοτε;   980

ΓΡ. οὐ πολλά· καὶ γὰρ ἐκνομίως μ᾽ ᾐσχύνετο.
ἀλλ᾽ ἀργυρίου δραχμὰς ἂν ᾔτησ᾽ εἴκοσιν
εἰς ἱμάτιον, ὀκτὼ δ᾽ ἂν εἰς ὑποδήματα·
καὶ ταῖς ἀδελφαῖς ἀγοράσαι χιτώνιον
ἐκέλευσεν ἄν, τῇ μητρί θ᾽ ἱματίδιον·   985
πυρῶν τ᾽ ἂν ἐδεήθη μεδίμνων τεττάρων.

ΧΡ. οὐ πολλὰ τοίνυν μὰ τὸν Ἀπόλλω ταῦτά γε
εἴρηκας, ἀλλὰ δῆλον ὅτι σ᾽ ᾐσχύνετο.

ΓΡ. καὶ ταῦτα τοίνυν οὐχ ἕνεκεν μισητίας
αἰτεῖν μ᾽ ἔφασκεν, ἀλλὰ φιλίας οὕνεκα,   990
ἵνα τοὐμὸν ἱμάτιον φορῶν μεμνῇτό μου.

ΧΡ. λέγεις ἐρῶντ᾽ ἄνθρωπον ἐκνομιώτατα.

ΓΡ. ἀλλ᾽ οὐχὶ νῦν ὁ βδελυρὸς ἔτι τὸν νοῦν ἔχει
τὸν αὐτὸν, ἀλλὰ πολὺ μεθέστηκεν πάνυ.
ἐμοῦ γὰρ αὐτῷ τὸν πλακοῦντα τουτονὶ   995
καὶ τἄλλα τἀπὶ τοῦ πίνακος τραγήματα
ἐπόντα πεμψάσης ὑπειπούσης θ᾽ ὅτι
εἰς ἑσπέραν ἥξοιμι, ΧΡ. τί σ᾽ ἔδρασ᾽; εἰπέ μοι.

ΓΡ. ἄμητα προσαπέπεμψεν ἡμῖν τουτονὶ,
ἐφ᾽ ᾧ τ᾽ ἐκεῖσε μηδέποτέ μ᾽ ἐλθεῖν ἔτι,   1000
καὶ πρὸς ἐπὶ τούτοις εἶπεν ἀποπέμπων ὅτι
πάλαι ποτ᾽ ἦσαν ἄλκιμοι Μιλήσιοι.

ΧΡ. δῆλον ὅτι τοὺς τρόπους τις οὐ μοχθηρὸς ἦν.
ἔπειτα πλουτῶν οὐκέθ᾽ ἥδεται φακῇ·

πρὸ τοῦ δ' ὑπὸ τῆς πενίας ἅπαντ' ἐπήσθιεν. 1005

ΓΡ. καὶ μὴν πρὸ τοῦ γ' ὁσημέραι νὴ τὼ θεὼ
ἐπὶ τὴν θύραν ἐβάδιζεν ἀεὶ τὴν ἐμήν.

ΧΡ. ἐπ' ἐκφοράν;

ΓΡ. μὰ Δί', ἀλλὰ τῆς φωνῆς μόνον
ἐρῶν ἀκοῦσαι. ΧΡ. τοῦ λαβεῖν μὲν οὖν χάριν.

ΓΡ. καὶ νὴ Δί' εἰ λυπουμένην αἴσθοιτό με, 1010
νηττάριον ἂν καὶ φάβιον ὑπεκορίζετο.

ΧΡ. ἔπειτ' ἴσως ᾔτησ' ἂν εἰς ὑποδήματα.

ΓΡ. μυστηρίοις δὲ τοῖς μεγάλοις ὀχουμένην
ἐπὶ τῆς ἁμάξης ὅτι προσέβλεψέν μέ τις,
ἐτυπτόμην διὰ τοῦθ' ὅλην τὴν ἡμέραν. 1015
οὕτω σφόδρα ζηλότυπος ὁ νεανίσκος ἦν.

ΧΡ. μόνος γὰρ ᾔδεθ', ὡς ἔοικεν, ἐσθίων.

ΓΡ. καὶ τάς γε χεῖρας παγκάλους ἔχειν μ' ἔφη.

ΧΡ. ὁπότε προτείνοιέν γε δραχμὰς εἴκοσιν.

ΓΡ. ὄζειν τε τῆς χρόας ἔφασκεν ἡδύ με, 1020

ΧΡ. εἰ Θάσιον ἐνέχεις, εἰκότως γε νὴ Δία.

ΓΡ. ταῦτ' οὖν ὁ θεός, ὦ φίλ' ἄνερ, οὐκ ὀρθῶς ποιεῖ,
φάσκων βοηθεῖν τοῖς ἀδικουμένοις ἀεί. 1025

ΧΡ. τί γὰρ ποιήσῃ; φράζε, καὶ πεπράξεται.

ΓΡ. ἀναγκάσαι δίκαιόν ἐστι νὴ Δία
τὸν εὖ παθόνθ' ὑπ' ἐμοῦ πάλιν μ' ἀντευποιεῖν·
ἢ μηδ' ὁτιοῦν ἀγαθὸν δίκαιός ἐστ' ἔχειν. 1030
ἀλλ' οὐδέποτέ με ζῶσαν ἀπολείψειν ἔφη.

ΧΡ. ὀρθῶς γε· νυνδί σ' οὐκέτι ζῆν οἴεται.

ΓΡ. ὑπὸ τοῦ γὰρ ἄλγους κατατέτηκ', ὦ φίλτατε.

ΧΡ. οὔκ, ἀλλὰ κατασέσηπας, ὥς γ' ἐμοὶ δοκεῖς. 1035

ΓΡ. διὰ δακτυλίου μὲν οὖν ἐμέ γ' ἂν διελκύσαις.

ΧΡ. εἰ τυγχάνοι γ' ὁ δακτύλιος ὢν τηλία.

ΓΡ. καὶ μὴν τὸ μειράκιον τοδὶ προσέρχεται,

οὕπερ πάλαι κατηγοροῦσα τυγχάνω·
ἔοικε δ' ἐπὶ κῶμον βαδίζειν.   1040
ΧΡ.   φαίνεται.
στεφάνους γέ τοι καὶ δᾷδ' ἔχων πορεύεται.
ΝΕΑ. ἀσπάζομαι   ΓΡ. τί φησιν;
ΝΕΑ.   ἀρχαίαν φίλην.
πολιὰ γεγένησαι ταχύ γε νὴ τὸν οὐρανόν.
ΓΡ. τάλαιν' ἐγὼ τῆς ὕβρεος ἧς ὑβρίζομαι.
ΧΡ. ἔοικε διὰ πολλοῦ χρόνου σ' ἑορακέναι.   1045
ΓΡ. ποίου χρόνου, ταλάνταθ', ὃς παρ' ἐμοὶ χθὲς ἦν;
ΧΡ. τοὐναντίον πέπονθε τοῖς πολλοῖς ἄρα·
μεθύων γὰρ, ὡς ἔοικεν, ὀξύτερον βλέπει.
ΓΡ. οὐκ, ἀλλ' ἀκόλαστός ἐστιν ἀεὶ τοὺς τρόπους.
ΝΕΑ. ὦ Ποντοπόσειδον καὶ θεοὶ πρεσβυτικοί,   1050
ἐν τῷ προσώπῳ τῶν ῥυτίδων ὅσας ἔχει.
ΓΡ. ἆ ἆ,
τὴν δᾷδα μή μοι πρόσφερ'.
ΧΡ.   εὖ μέντοι λέγει.
ἐὰν γὰρ αὐτὴν εἷς μόνος σπινθὴρ λάβῃ,
ὥσπερ παλαιὰν εἰρεσιώνην καύσεται.
ΝΕΑ. βούλει διὰ χρόνου πρός με παῖσαι;   ΓΡ. ποῦ,
     τάλαν;   1055
ΝΕΑ. αὐτοῦ, λαβοῦσα κάρυα.   ΓΡ. παιδιὰν τίνα;
ΝΕΑ. πόσους ἔχεις ὀδόντας.
ΧΡ.   ἀλλὰ γνώσομαι
κἄγωγ'· ἔχει γὰρ τρεῖς ἴσως ἢ τέτταρας.
ΝΕΑ. ἀπότισον· ἕνα γὰρ γόμφιον μόνον φορεῖ.
ΓΡ. ταλάντατ' ἀνδρῶν, οὐχ ὑγιαίνειν μοι δοκεῖς,   1060
πλυνόν με ποιῶν ἐν τοσούτοις ἀνδράσιν.
ΝΕΑ. ὄναιο μέντἂν, εἴ τις ἐκπλύνειέ σε.
ΧΡ. οὐ δῆτ', ἐπεὶ νῦν μὲν καπηλικῶς ἔχει,

εἰ δ' ἐκπλυνεῖται τοῦτο τὸ ψιμύθιον,
ὄψει κατάδηλα τοῦ προσώπου τὰ ῥάκη.　1065
ΓΡ. γέρων ἀνὴρ ὢν οὐχ ὑγιαίνειν μοι δοκεῖς.
ΧΡ. ἀλλ', ὦ νεανίσκ', οὐκ ἐῶ τὴν μείρακα
μισεῖν σε ταύτην. ΝΕΑ. ἀλλ' ἔγωγ' ὑπερφιλῶ.
ΧΡ. καὶ μὴν κατηγορεῖ γέ σου. ΝΕΑ. τί κατηγορεῖ;
ΧΡ. εἶναί σ' ὑβριστήν φησι καὶ λέγειν ὅτι
πάλαι ποτ' ἦσαν ἄλκιμοι Μιλήσιοι.　1075
ΝΕΑ. ἐγὼ περὶ ταύτης οὐ μαχοῦμαί σοι. ΧΡ. τὸ τί;
ΝΕΑ. αἰσχυνόμενος τὴν ἡλικίαν τὴν σήν, ἐπεὶ
οὐκ ἄν ποτ' ἄλλῳ τοῦτό γ' ἐπέτρεπον ποιεῖν·
νῦν δ' ἄπιθι χαίρων συλλαβὼν τὴν μείρακα.
ἀλλ' εἴσιθ' εἴσω· τῷ θεῷ γὰρ βούλομαι
ἐλθὼν ἀναθεῖναι τοὺς στεφάνους τούσδ' οὓς ἔχω.
ΓΡ. ἐγὼ δέ γ' αὐτῷ καὶ φράσαι τι βούλομαι.　1090
ΝΕΑ. ἐγὼ δέ γ' οὐκ εἴσειμι.
ΧΡ.　　　　θάρρει, μὴ φοβοῦ.
οὐ γὰρ βιάσεται.
ΝΕΑ.　　　　πάνυ καλῶς τοίνυν λέγεις.
ΓΡ. βάδιζ'· ἐγὼ δέ σου κατόπιν εἰσέρχομαι.
ΧΡ. ὡς εὐτόνως, ὦ Ζεῦ βασιλεῦ, τὸ γρᾴδιον　1095
ὥσπερ λεπὰς τῷ μειρακίῳ προσίσχεται.
ΚΑ. τίς ἔσθ' ὁ κόπτων τὴν θύραν; τουτὶ τί ἦν;
οὐδεὶς ἔοικεν· ἀλλὰ δῆτα τὸ θύριον
φθεγγόμενον ἄλλως κλαυσιᾷ.
ΕΡ.　　　　σέ τοι λέγω,
ὦ Καρίων, ἀνάμεινον.　1100
ΚΑ.　　　　οὗτος, εἰπέ μοι,
σὺ τὴν θύραν ἔκοπτες οὑτωσὶ σφόδρα;
ΕΡ. μὰ Δί', ἀλλ' ἔμελλον· εἶτ' ἀνέῳξάς με φθάσας.
ἀλλ' ἐκκάλει τὸν δεσπότην τρέχων ταχύ,

ἔπειτα τὴν γυναῖκα καὶ τὰ παιδία,
ἔπειτα τοὺς θεράποντας, εἶτα τὴν κύνα, 1105
ἔπειτα σαυτόν, εἶτα τὴν ὗν.

ΚΑ. εἰπέ μοι,
τί δ᾽ ἔστιν;

ΕΡ. ὁ Ζεὺς, ὦ πονηρὲ, βούλεται
ἐς ταυτὸν ὑμᾶς συγκυκήσας τρυβλίον
ἀπαξάπαντας εἰς τὸ βάραθρον ἐμβαλεῖν.

ΚΑ. ἡ γλῶττα τῷ κήρυκι τούτων τέμνεται. 1110
ἀτὰρ τιὴ δὴ ταῦτ᾽ ἐπιβουλεύει ποιεῖν
ἡμᾶς;

ΕΡ. ὅτιη δεινότατα πάντων πραγμάτων
εἴργασθ᾽. ἀφ᾽ οὗ γὰρ ἤρξατ᾽ ἐξ ἀρχῆς βλέπειν
ὁ Πλοῦτος, οὐδεὶς οὐ λιβανωτὸν, οὐ δάφνην,
οὐ ψαιστὸν, οὐχ ἱερεῖον, οὐκ ἄλλ᾽ οὐδεὲν 1115
ἡμῖν ἔτι θύει τοῖς θεοῖς.

ΚΑ. μὰ Δί᾽, οὐδέ γε
θύσει. κακῶς γὰρ ἐπεμελεῖσθ᾽ ἡμῶν τότε.

ΕΡ. καὶ τῶν μὲν ἄλλων μοι θεῶν ἧττον μέλει,
ἐγὼ δ᾽ ἀπόλωλα κἀπιτέτριμμαι. ΚΑ. σωφρονεῖς.

ΕΡ. πρότερον γὰρ εἶχον μὲν παρὰ ταῖς καπηλίσιν 1120
πάντ᾽ ἀγάθ᾽ ἕωθεν εὐθὺς, οἰνοῦτταν, μέλι,
ἰσχάδας, ὅσ᾽ εἰκὸς ἐστιν Ἑρμῆν ἐσθίειν·
νυνὶ δὲ πεινῶν ἀναβάδην ἀναπαύομαι.

ΚΑ. οὔκουν δικαίως, ὅστις ἐποίεις ζημίαν
ἐνίοτε τοιαῦτ᾽ ἀγάθ᾽ ἔχων; 1125

ΕΡ. οἴμοι τάλας,
οἴμοι πλακοῦντος τοῦ 'ν τετράδι πεπεμμένου.

ΚΑ. ποθεῖς τὸν οὐ παρόντα καὶ μάτην καλεῖς.

ΕΡ. οἴμοι δὲ κωλῆς ἧς ἐγὼ κατήσθιον·

ΚΑ. ἀσκωλίαζ᾽ ἐνταῦθα πρὸς τὴν αἰθρίαν.

ΕΡ. σπλάγχνων τε θερμῶν ὧν ἐγὼ κατήσθιον. 1130
ΚΑ. ὀδύνη σε περὶ τὰ σπλάγχν' ἔοικέ τις στρέφειν.
ΕΡ. οἴμοι δὲ κύλικος ἴσον ἴσῳ κεκραμένης.
ΚΑ. ταύτην ἐπιπιὼν ἀποτρέχων οὐκ ἂν φθάνοις;
ΕΡ. ἆρ' ὠφελήσαις ἄν τι τὸν σαυτοῦ φίλον;
ΚΑ. εἴ του δέει γ' ὧν δυνατός εἰμί σ' ὠφελεῖν. 1135
ΕΡ. εἴ μοι πορίσας ἄρτον τιν' εὖ πεπεμμένον
δοίης καταφαγεῖν καὶ κρέας νεανικὸν
ὧν θύεθ' ὑμεῖς ἔνδον. ΚΑ. ἀλλ' οὐκ ἐκφορά.
ΕΡ. καὶ μὴν ὁπότε τι σκευάριον τοῦ δεσπότου
ὑφέλοι', ἐγώ σ' ἂν λανθάνειν ἐποίουν ἀεί. 1140
ΚΑ. ἐφ' ᾧ τε μετέχειν καὐτός, ὦ τοιχωρύχε.
ἧκεν γὰρ ἄν σοι ναστὸς εὖ πεπεμμένος.
ΕΡ. ἔπειτα τοῦτόν γ' αὐτὸς ἂν κατήσθιες.
ΚΑ. οὐ γὰρ μετεῖχες τὰς ἴσας πληγὰς ἐμοί,
ὁπότε τι ληφθείην πανουργήσας ἐγώ. 1145
ΕΡ. μὴ μνησικακήσῃς, εἰ σὺ Φυλὴν κατέλαβες.
ἀλλὰ ξύνοικον πρὸς θεῶν δέξασθέ με.
ΚΑ. ἔπειτ' ἀπολιπὼν τοὺς θεοὺς ἐνθάδε μενεῖς;
ΕΡ. τὰ γὰρ παρ' ὑμῖν ἐστι βελτίω πολύ.
ΚΑ. τί δέ; ταὐτομολεῖν ἀστεῖον εἶναί σοι δοκεῖ; 1150
ΕΡ. πατρὶς γάρ ἐστι πᾶσ' ἵν' ἂν πράττῃ τις εὖ.
ΚΑ. τί δῆτ' ἂν εἴης ὄφελος ἡμῖν ἐνθάδ' ὤν;
ΕΡ. παρὰ τὴν θύραν στροφαῖον ἱδρύσασθέ με.
ΚΑ. στροφαῖον; ἀλλ' οὐκ ἔργον ἔστ' οὐδὲν στροφῶν.
ΕΡ. ἀλλ' ἐμπολαῖον. 1155
ΚΑ.   ἀλλὰ πλουτοῦμεν· τί οὖν
Ἑρμῆν παλιγκάπηλον ἡμᾶς δεῖ τρέφειν;
ΕΡ. ἀλλὰ δόλιον τοίνυν.
ΚΑ.   δόλιον; ἥκιστά γε·
οὐ γὰρ δόλου νῦν ἔργον, ἀλλ' ἁπλῶν τρόπων.

ΕΡ. ἀλλ' ἡγεμόνιον.

ΚΑ.　　　　　　　ἀλλ' ὁ θεὸς ἤδη βλέπει,
ὥσθ' ἡγεμόνος οὐδὲν δεησόμεσθ' ἔτι.　　1160

ΕΡ. ἐναγώνιος τοίνυν ἔσομαι. καὶ τί ἔτ' ἐρεῖς;
Πλούτῳ γάρ ἐστι τοῦτο συμφορώτατον,
ποιεῖν ἀγῶνας μουσικοὺς καὶ γυμνικούς.

ΚΑ. ὡς ἀγαθόν ἐστ' ἐπωνυμίας πολλὰς ἔχειν·
οὗτος γὰρ ἐξεύρηκεν αὐτῷ βιότιον.　　1165
οὐκ ἐτὸς ἅπαντες οἱ δικάζοντες θαμὰ
σπεύδουσιν ἐν πολλοῖς γεγράφθαι γράμμασιν.

ΕΡ. οὐκοῦν ἐπὶ τούτοις εἰσίω;

ΚΑ.　　　　　　　καὶ πλῦνέ γε
αὐτὸς προσελθὼν πρὸς τὸ φρέαρ τὰς κοιλίας,
ἵν' εὐθέως διακονικὸς εἶναι δοκῇς.　　1170

ΙΕ. τίς ἂν φράσειε ποῦ 'στι Χρεμύλος μοι σαφῶς;

ΧΡ. τί δ' ἔστιν, ὦ βέλτιστε;

ΙΕ.　　　　　　　τί γὰρ ἀλλ' ἢ κακῶς;
ἀφ' οὗ γὰρ ὁ Πλοῦτος οὗτος ἤρξατο βλέπειν,
ἀπόλωλ' ὑπὸ λιμοῦ. καταφαγεῖν γὰρ οὐκ ἔχω,
καὶ ταῦτα τοῦ σωτῆρος ἱερεὺς ὢν Διός.　　1175

ΧΡ. ἡ δ' αἰτία τίς ἐστιν, ὦ πρὸς τῶν θεῶν;

ΙΕ. θύειν ἔτ' οὐδεὶς ἀξιοῖ. ΧΡ. τίνος οὕνεκα;

ΙΕ. ὅτι πάντες εἰσὶ πλούσιοι· καίτοι τότε,
ὅτ' εἶχον οὐδὲν, ὁ μὲν ἂν ἥκων ἔμπορος
ἔθυσεν ἱερεῖόν τι σωθείς, ὁ δέ τις ἂν　　1180
δίκην ἀποφυγών· ὁ δ' ἂν ἐκαλλιερεῖτό τις,
κἀμέ γ' ἐκάλει τὸν ἱερέα· νῦν δ' οὐδὲ εἷς
θύει τὸ παράπαν οὐδὲν, οὐδ' εἰσέρχεται.
τὸν οὖν Δία τὸν σωτῆρα καὐτός μοι δοκῶ　　1186
χαίρειν ἐάσας ἐνθάδ' αὐτοῦ καταμενεῖν.

ΧΡ. θάρρει· καλῶς ἔσται γάρ, ἢν θεὸς θέλῃ.

ὁ Ζεὺς ὁ σωτὴρ γὰρ πάρεστιν ἐνθάδε,
αὐτόματος ἥκων. ΙΕ. πάντ' ἀγαθὰ τοίνυν λέγεις.

ΧΡ. ἱδρυσόμεθ' οὖν αὐτίκα μάλ', ἀλλὰ περίμενε,   1191
τὸν Πλοῦτον, οὗπερ πρότερον ἦν ἱδρυμένος,
τὸν ὀπισθόδομον ἀεὶ φυλάττων τῆς θεοῦ.
ἀλλ' ἐκδότω τις δεῦρο δᾷδας ἡμμένας,
ἵν' ἔχων προηγῇ τῷ θεῷ σύ.   1195

ΙΕ.   πάνυ μὲν οὖν
δρᾶν ταῦτα χρή. ΧΡ. τὸν Πλοῦτον ἔξω τις κάλει.

ΓΡ. ἐγὼ δὲ τί ποιῶ;

ΧΡ.   τὰς χύτρας, αἷς τὸν θεὸν
ἱδρυσόμεθα, λαβοῦσ' ἐπὶ τῆς κεφαλῆς φέρε
σεμνῶς· ἔχουσα δ' ἦλθες αὐτὴ ποικίλα.

ΓΡ. ὧν δ' οὕνεκ' ἦλθον;   1200

ΧΡ.   πάντα σοι πεπράξεται.
ἥξει γὰρ ὁ νεανίσκος ὥς σ' εἰς ἑσπέραν.

ΓΡ. ἀλλ' εἴ γε μέντοι νὴ Δί' ἐγγυᾷ σύ μοι
ἥξειν ἐκεῖνον ὡς ἔμ', οἴσω τὰς χύτρας.

ΧΡ. καὶ μὴν πολὺ τῶν ἄλλων χυτρῶν τἀναντία
αὗται ποιοῦσι· ταῖς μὲν ἄλλαις γὰρ χύτραις   1205
ἡ γραῦς ἔπεστ' ἀνωτάτω, ταύτης δὲ νῦν
τῆς γραὸς ἐπιπολῆς ἔπεισιν αἱ χύτραι.

ΧΟ. οὐκ ἔτι τοίνυν εἰκὸς μέλλειν οὐδ' ἡμᾶς, ἀλλ' ἀνα-
χωρεῖν
εἰς τοὔπισθεν· δεῖ γὰρ κατόπιν τούτων ᾄδοντας
ἕπεσθαι.

NOTES.

1—21. Carion the slave of Chremylus complains of his hard lot as slave of a crazy master, who follows a blind man for no apparent reason. He resolves to make Chremylus explain why he does so.

2. παραφρονοῦντος] So in the *Peace* the master Trygaeus is crazy (1. 54) and in the *Wasps* Bdelycleon: and their slaves talk of them. Indeed the slave of comedy is constantly better than his master in common sense.

5. μετέχειν κ.τ.λ.] The master foolishly will not take the slave's advice, gets into a scrape, and the slave shares it. The word μετέχειν shows that this is chiefly meant, not that the slave gets beaten : though this may happen too, for the master may revenge himself for his own fault on the slave's back. Any excuse would do for a beating, cf. *Ran.* 812 ὁπόταν οἱ δεσπόται ἐσπουδάκωσι κλαύμαθ᾽ ἡμῖν γίγνεται.

6. τὸν κύριον] 'Its natural owner,' that is, the slave himself. τὸν ἐωνημένον the master who has bought him.

8. καὶ ταῦτα...ταῦτα] 'And these things are thus :' a common phrase when one subject is dismissed and the speaker passes on to something else. Cf. Aesch. *Prom. Vinct.* 508 τοιαῦτα μὲν δὴ ταῦτα.

9. ὃς θεσπιῳδεῖ] A line of tragic sound.

12. μελαγχολῶντ᾽] Cf. *Av.* 14 ὁ πινακοπώλης Φιλοκράτης μελαγχολῶν, and below l. 903.

16. ἀκολουθεῖ κ.τ.λ.] Chremylus follows a blind man and forces me to do so too.

17. ἀποκρινομένῳ] 'And that too though he (the old man) answers not one syllable.' Bentley's ἀποκρινόμενος, which Meineke and Holden accept, for ἀποκρινομένῳ the Ravenna MS. reading, appears needless. We may well suppose Plutus to have been already questioned by Carion or Chremylus : the threat in l. 57 rather implies this. And it is far more to the purpose for Carion in describing his master's craziness to say 'he follows a blind man, aye and one who won't answer him,' than to say, 'he follows a blind man and he won't tell me why.' The common MS. reading ἀποκρινομένου might be defended, as genitive absolute. Dindorf's older text (from Rav. MS.) ἀποκρινομένῳ has been kept. The dative is governed by ἀκολουθεῖ.

οὐδὲ γρῦ] Besides the accepted explanation of 'a grunt,' whence comes γρύζειν, the Scholiast gives another, that γρῦ means ῥύπος ὄνυχος, and hence anything worthless and small. The expression οὐδὲ γρῦ occurs in Demosth. 353. Cf. *Ran.* 913, *Eq.* 294 in support of the usual explanation.

21. στέφανον ἔχοντά γε] Those returning from an oracle wore a wreath, and their persons were sacred.

22—55. Chremylus tells Carion that, finding himself and other honest folk poor while rascals were rich, he went to Apollo to seek a remedy. The god told him to follow the first person he met after leaving the temple and to persuade him to go home with him. He had met this blind man, and therefore he stuck to him. They must now find out who he is.

27. κλεπτίστατον] A comic surprise and contradiction after πιστότατον. The superlative form is wrongly compared by Bergler to τολμίστατος Soph. *Philoct.* 984, for τολμήστατος is there the true reading, which from τολμήεις is regular. Similar forms are λαλίστερος, ἁρπαγίστατος, ὀψοφαγίστατος.

30. ῥήτορες] Cf. below l. 379, 566. Aristophanes often attacks this class.

33. τὸν ἐμὸν κ.τ.λ.] He consulted the god not for his own benefit so much, as his life was well-nigh spent, but for his son's, to ask what kind of life he ought to lead.

34. ἐκτετοξεῦσθαι] 'to have been already shot away, spent:' the metaphor is from the arrows being all shot and the quiver emptied. Life itself is conceived as made up of arrows. 'The arrows of my life,' says Chremylus, 'are well-nigh shot out.' Spanheim compares Hor. *Od.* ii. 16, 17 Quid brevi fortes jaculamur aevo multa? but it is not quite the same use of the metaphor. Bentley's conjecture ἐκτετολυπεῦσθαι will find few supporters, though it is ingenious.

35. τὸν υἱόν] Governed grammatically by χρή, but put first in the sentence in order to contrast with τὸν ἐμὸν μὲν βίον.

37. ὑγιὲς μηδὲ ἕν] 'an utterly dishonest creature, a good-for-nothing.' Some write μηδεὲν here, as οὐδεὲν in l. 137 and οὐδεεὶς in l. 1182. Whichever way it be written, the separation of the syllables makes the word more emphatic than οὐδεὶς, οὐδέν.

39. τί δῆτα] A line of tragic sound. The tripod and the priestess were wreathed with bay.

44. καὶ τῷ κ.τ.λ.] 'And pray whom do you meet first?' 'This man.' 'Then don't you understand etc.' For καὶ τῷ Meineke says "κᾆτα recte Cobetus, τουτῳὶ Carioni continuans." What objection is there to the common text? And εἶτα in l. 45 comes very awkwardly after κᾆτα when the whole is Carion's speech.

45. τὴν ἐπίνοιαν] The meaning of the god is to tell you that your son should practise the national trade of knavery. For that knavery pays now-a-days even a blind man can see.

47. τὸν ἐπιχώριον τ.] Cf. *Nub.* 1173 τοῦτο τοὐπιχώριον ἀτεχνῶς ἐπανθεῖ.

48. δῆλον ὁτιὴ κ.τ.λ.] The right construction of this appears to be ὁτιὴ τοῦτο δοκεῖ δῆλον καὶ τυφλῷ γνῶναι, 'because this seems plain even for a blind man to discern.' Comp. below l. 489 φανερὸν οἶμαι τοῦτ' εἶναι πᾶσι γνῶναι. This use of ὁτιὴ 'Because' to begin an answer is supported by other passages. Cf. *Nub.* 755 ὁτιὴ τί δή; ὁτιὴ κ.τ.λ. 'Why so pray?' 'Because etc.' And so here: 'How do you make out that?' 'Because etc.' Meineke proposes γνωστὸν in his critical note. In the *Vindiciae* he attempts other changes which are not satisfactory. If δῆλον ὁτιὴ be taken together as δηλονότι, it is hardly possible to explain δοκεῖ. Meineke argues that δῆλον ὅτι cannot be divorced: true, if ὅτι means 'that,' of fact; but ὁτιὴ appears only to be used = 'because,' of reason.

52. ἦν δ' ἡμῖν κ.τ.λ.] Something more must be meant than what Carion supposes : this might be found out, if the old man would say who he is. This and the following speech of Carion quite agree with the supposition that Plutus had been already questioned by Chremylus or Carion, and support the MS. reading in l. 17.

56—252. The old man reluctantly, after severe threats, tells them that he is Plutus, and explains his blindness. Chremylus proposes to restore him to sight ; shows that he will be supreme above all deities, and need not fear the anger of Zeus. He persuades Plutus to consent to this and to go home with him, promising him better treatment than he has hitherto met with. Meanwhile Carion is sent to summon the friends of Chremylus.

57. τἀπὶ τούτοις] i. e. blows and stripes. δρῶ is deliberative subj. 'am I to do?'

58. μανθάνεις] Carion affects to misunderstand Plutus' answer, 'You must say who you are.' 'I say to you, Go and be hanged.' 'Do you understand who he says he is?'

60. σκαιῶς κ.τ.λ.] 'You are not polite enough,' says Chremylus ; and then turning to Plutus he courteously entreats him: but he gets much the same answer.

61. εἴ τι...τρόποις] 'if you like an honest man, answer *me*, for I am one.' Or 'if you take pleasure in honesty, if you are yourself an honest man.' Perhaps this last is better, for so in the next line τὸν ἄνδρα will have more force.

63. δέχου τὸν ἄνδρα] 'There, take your man and the omen that the god gives you.' Chremylus had adjured him to speak 'as he was a true man.' Carion ironically tells his master to take and make the most of 'his true man.' And Plutus who had first met C. on leaving the oracle was to be regarded as an omen or ὄρνις. Cf. *Av.* 719 ὄρνιν

τε νομίζετε πάνθ᾽ ὅσαπερ περὶ μαντείας διακρίνει...ξύμβολον ὄρνιν, φωνὴν ὄρνιν.

65. ἀπό σ᾽ ὀλῶ] i. e. ἀπολῶ σε.

66. ὦ τᾶν] The Scholiast quotes from Cratinus ὦ τᾶν ἐθελήσετε. Probably in strictness τᾶν is singular, and is spoken only to Chremylus: ' My good sir.' Then he adds ' do leave me both of you.'

πώμαλα] This negative = οὐδαμῶς was no doubt originally an interrogative from πῶ = ποῦ. So also πόθεν is used : ' how can it be?' meaning ' it cannot be.'

70. ἐκτραχηλισθῇ π.] Cf. *Nub.* 1501 ἐκτραχηλισθῶ πεσών: also *Lys.* 705. The active ἐκτραχηλίζειν is used by Xenophon of a horse that throws his rider over his head. Fischer thinks that Aristophanes' use of the word for ' to break the neck' comes from the other use, "because riders who are so thrown frequently break their own necks." Doubtless the two meanings are independent of each other, both coming naturally from the word.

71. αἷρε] Cf *Eq.* 1361 ἄρας μετέωρον εἰς τὸ βάραθρον ἐμβαλῶ.

74. νὴ τοὺς θεούς] An assent to what οὐκ ἀφήσετον suggests. ' Yes, by the gods, we will let you go, at least if you wish to be let go.' They do not however let him go (see below l. 101), but eventually they reconcile him to the idea of remaining with them.

75. μέθεσθέ] They had been holding him. For ἦν = ἰδοὺ cf. *Eq.* 26, *Ran.* 1390, *Pac.* 327.

77. ἦ] 1st pers. sing., as the Scholiast notes.

79. ἀνδρῶν] As in *Av.* 1637, *Ran.* 1472 ἀνθρώπων addressed to Poseidon and Dionysus.

83. αὐτότατος] 'ipsissimus,' 'his selfest self.' Kuster quotes from Plautus' Trinummus iv. 2 : ' Syc. Ain' tu tandem? is ipsusne es? Ch. Aio. Syc. Ipsus es? Ch. Ipsus, inquam, Charmides sum. Syc. Ergo ipsusne es? Ch. Ipsissumus.'

84. Πατροκλέους] A rich man who followed Laconian fashions, the Scholiast says. In Plato's *Euthydemus*, p. 297, Socrates speaks of a brother of his named Patrocles. What the Laconian and Socratic habits were Aristophanes tells us in *Av.* 1281 ἐλακωνομάχουν ἅπαντες ἄνθρωποι τότε, ἐκόμων ἐπείνων ἐρρύπων ἐσωκράτων. Whereas with the Athenians washings were frequent : especially before and after meals ; cf. *Vesp.* 1216.

86. τουτί] i.e. blindness.

92. φθονεῖ] This jealousy was often attributed by the ancient heathen to their gods.

93. καὶ μήν] Yet it is very unfair that Zeus should grudge prosperity to the good, for it is owing to the good (διὰ τοὺς χρ.) that he gets honours.

98. ἑόρακα διά] The MS. ἑώρακά πω cannot be right : οὔπω means ' nondum,' ' not yet:' and the sense wanted is ' I have not now for a

long time seen.' Porson proposed ἑώρακ' ἀπὸ χρόνου. If a preposition be inserted διὰ seems the neatest for the sense: cf. below 1045 ἔοικε διὰ πολλοῦ χρόνου σ' ἑορακέναι. Brunck proposed ἑώρων διὰ χρόνου: but there seems no need to change the tense.

99. οὐδ' ἐγώ] Even with eyes it is hard to find honest men at Athens.

100. τἀπ' ἐμοῦ] Dindorf blames a brother commentator for supposing this to be τὰ ἀπὸ, and affirms it to be τὰ ἐπί. It may be either: 'all that concerns me, all my case:' or 'all that you can hear from me, all my story.' The latter is at least as likely as the former.

106. οὐ γὰρ ἔστιν κ.τ.λ.] There lives no other save myself who is as honest as I.

107. ταυτὶ κ.τ.λ.] All, when poor, profess goodness, but, once rich, they turn bad.

111. οἰμώξει] Carion is impatient with Plutus, and would fain return to the argument of force which he proposed above, l. 57, 65.

114. σὺν θεῷ δ' εἰρ.] Cf. Eur. *Med.* 625 ἴσως γὰρ, ξὺν θεῷ δ' εἰρήσεται, γαμεῖς τοιοῦτον ὥστε σ' ἀρνεῖσθαι γάμον.

115. ὀφθαλμίας] Generally of the 'lippitudo' to which the Athenians were very liable: so also is used the verb ὀφθαλμιᾶν. Here it=τυφλότης: but to understate the evil is courtesy on Chremylus' part.

118. ἄθλιος φ.] 'By nature wretched,' because he wilfully chooses to remain blind.

119. ὁ Ζεὺς μὲν οὖν] Nay, it is not wilful folly, but fear of Zeus. The order of the words is somewhat involved, οἶδα ὡς ὁ Ζεὺς ἐπιτρίψειεν ἂν ἐμὲ εἰ πύθοιτο τὰ τούτων μῶρα, 'if Zeus were to hear their folly (the proposal to restore my sight) he would destroy me.' To which Chremylus replies that Plutus cannot be worse destroyed than he is, stumbling about blindly. Meineke proposes ἰδών for οἶδ' ὡς, which last is an alteration of MS. εἰδώς. ἰδών would govern μῶρα, ἐμὲ would be governed by πύθοιτο and ἐπιτρίψειε.

120. τοῦτο δρᾷ] i.e. ἐπιτρίβει. To Epops, when he enters in sorry plight (*Av.* 95), Euelpides says οἱ δώδεκα θεοὶ εἴξασιν ἐπιτρῖψαί σε.

127. ἄ] Plutus is shocked at Chremylus' audacity.

129. ἐμὲ σύ ;] In repeating questions like this the Greeks repeat the pronoun, but in English we should repeat and emphasize some other word. 'I'll prove you more powerful than Zeus.' 'You will?' or 'More powerful than Zeus?' Cf. *Av.* 467 and the note there.

130. αὐτίκα] Cf. note on *Av.* 166.

134. ἄντικρυς] 'straight out, plainly.' So Juvenal says, 'Prima fere vota et cunctis notissima templis Divitiae.'

138. ψαιστὸν] ἄλευρον ἐλαίῳ δεδευμένον Schol. Again used below, l. 1115.

4—2

142. ἦν λυπῇ] i.e. ἦν ὁ Ζεὺς σὲ λυπῇ. Cf. *Av.* 1246 Ζεὺς εἴ με λυπήσει πέρα where Peisthetaerus is mocking at Zeus.

147. μ. ἀργυρίδιον] A contemptuous diminutive 'just for a paltry little sum of money.'

160. τέχναι] This list of trades Meineke divides between Chremylus and Carion: and so again l. 170—80.

165. λωποδυτεῖ] Clothes-stealer and housebreaker come in comically in the middle of the trades.

166. γναφεύει] κναφεύει was read by the Scholiast, who tells us that κν was older Attic, γν newer. Meineke edits κναφεὺς in *Vesp.* 1128 *Eccl.* 415. ὁ δὲ κναφεύει would be against comic usage, as the ε should be short before -κν. Brunck proposed ὁ δέ τις κναφεύει γ', which some editors receive. It is hard to pronounce authoritatively which correction is the better, or whether either is needed. The metrical canon does not perhaps justify us in changing the MS. ὁ δὲ κναφεύει, for there are offences against it elsewhere. And the pronunciation and writing may have been in Aristophanes' later years (to which this play belongs) wavering between the κν and γν.

169. ταυτί μ' ἐλ.] All this Plutus had never noticed; nor knew how all-powerful he was.

170. διὰ τοῦτον] According to the common text Carion speaks to Chremylus; then in some lines addresses Plutus directly. Meineke and Brunck give lines alternately to servant and master. It appears best to give l. 172 and l. 177—9 to Chremylus. Thus Chremylus consistently addresses Plutus throughout, Carion speaks of him to Chremylus. It is plain that Carion must say ὁ Τιμοθέου δὲ πύργος and his master ἐμπέσοι γέ σοι.

κομᾷ] Metaphorical, as in *Vesp.* 1317. In *Eq.* 580 literal. The Persian king is proud because he is so rich.

171. διὰ τοῦτον] To get wealth: to save our own or appropriate that of others. Schol. Also the citizens received pay for attendance at the assembly.

173. ἐν Κ. ξενικὸν] The Thebans, Argives and Corinthians were leagued with Athens against the Lacedaemonians, and Corinth was the scene of operations.

174. Πάμφιλος] A demagogue who appropriated public money and was punished for it. And 'the needle-seller' was a hanger-on of this same Pamphilus. Schol.

177. Φιλέψιος] He got his livelihood (says the Scholiast) by reciting stories, in which he dealt in the marvellous. Demosthenes mentions a Philepsius among others who had been punished for breach of the law. c. *Timocr.* 742. He is there mentioned with Agyrrhius, for whom cf. *Eccles.* 96, 184.

178. ἡ ξυμμαχία κ.τ.λ.] Some alliance between Athens and Egypt, when the Athenians needed corn from Egypt and paid for it. But when this was is uncertain. The Scholiast speaks of it as in the reign of

Amasis, which is far too early. And Chabrias' visit to Egypt, which some have thought to be meant, was long after even the second exhibition of this play.

179. Φιλωνίδου] A rich man but of no beauty.

180. Τιμοθέου] Timotheus son of Conon built a tower, at great expense apparently. Carion would have completed his sentence 'was it not built through you?' but his master breaks in.

182. μονώτατος] Cf. l. 83 εὐτότατος.

185. ἐπικαθέζηται] This may be a metaphor from weighing: 'in whose scale wealth sits,' the depression of the scale being taken to indicate success. So the Scholiast interprets. The notion of the issue of battle represented by the turn of the scale is familiar to us. But in both cases in Homer, *Il.* θ. 69 and χ. 209, the scale of the vanquished sinks, of the victor rises. So too in Virgil, *Aen.* XII. 725. Milton makes the light scale of the weaker 'fly up and kick the beam.' But that the metaphor is from a balance here seems not so sure. Aristophanes himself uses ἐπικαθῆσθαι in *Eq.* 1093 of the owl perched on Athene's shoulder. Perhaps here Wealth is imagined as perching on the victor, much as the raven on Valerius in the Roman legend.

188. μεστὸς] 'too full, full to overflowing:' the force of this word is seen well in *Eq.* 814 ὃς ἐποίησεν τὴν πόλιν ἡμῶν μεστήν, εὑρὼν ἐπιχειλῆ.

189—93. Chremylus' list is of the higher pleasures, Carion's of the lowest bodily enjoyments, ridiculously specified. The sentiment with which Chremylus begins occurs in Homer *Il.* V. 636 πάντων μὲν κόρος ἐστι κ.τ.λ.

199. ἐν μόνον δ.] Plutus is modest about his own powers, as is the sausage-seller in the *Knights.*

200. δύναμιν] Attraction to the relative has changed the case : the sense is ταύτης τῆς δυνάμεως δεσπότης γενήσομαι ἥν φατε.

202. νὴ τὸν Δί'· ἀλλά] 'Yes, by Zeus ; you're doubtless afraid : nay 'tis even a proverb.' For the neuter δειλότατον comp. *Ran.* 282 οὐδὲν γὰρ οὕτω γαῦρόν ἐσθ' ὡς Ἡρακλῆς. And the very proverb alluded to is in Eur. *Phoen.* 597 δειλὸν δ' ὁ πλοῦτος καὶ φιλόψυχον κακόν.

204. ἐσδὺς] Join with ἐς τὴν οἰκίαν.

207. πρόνοιαν] Forethought or discretion we all know to be the better part of valour.

210. Λυγκέως] A proverb for keen sight : the Scholiast supposes Lynceus to have penetrated with lamps underground in mining operations.

213. σείσας δάφνην] 'Pythia, quae tripodi e Phoebi lauroque profatur.' Lucr. I. 739. 'Tremere omnia visa repente liminaque laurusque dei.' Virg. *Aen.* III. 90. Cf. above l. 39.

215. ὁρᾶτε] Whatever Plutus' 'take care' was meant for, Chremylus stops by μὴ φρόντιζε.

216. κἂν δῆ] χρῆ, Meineke, Holden. For sense δῆ=δέῃ seems the better: but the contraction is doubtful. Perhaps δέῃ pronounced as one syllable would be better.

220. πονηρούς γ'] A sorry lot of allies, these hungry fellows. They won't be so, says Chremylus, when they get their deserts and are rich.

227. καὶ δὴ] 'Even now.' For τουτοδὶ=τουτὶ δὲ cf. *Av.* 18 τηνδεδὶ, *Eq.* 1302 νυνδί.

κρεάδιον] The meat from the sacrifice: they were returning from Delphi.

233. καὶ δικαίως κἀδίκως] As Chremylus is χρηστὸς and δίκαιος the sense of ἀδίκως need not be pressed: the two adverbs mean 'in every possible way.' But it may perhaps be thought that in view of sudden wealth Chremylus has already become partially corrupted and forgets honesty.

234. ἀλλ' ἄχθομαι] 'I don't like going into a strange house: I either get buried or squandered,' says Plutus. In Lucian's *Timon* he complains much in the same style: ταῦτα καὶ αὐτὸς ἀγανακτῶ πρὸς ἐνίων μὲν ἀτίμως λακτιζόμενος καὶ λαφυσσόμενος καὶ ἐξαντλούμενος, ὑπ' ἐνίων δὲ ὥσπερ στιγματίας δραπέτης πεπεδημένος.

235. πάνυ] In sense belongs to the verb ἄχθομαι.

236. αὑτοῦ] τοῦ εἰσιέναι.

242. παραπλῆγ'] ἄφρονα, μανικόν. Cf. Soph. *Aj.* 230 παραπλήκτῳ χερί.

244. ἐν ἀκαρεῖ] ἀκαρῆ is used in *Vesp.* 541, 701, *Nub.* 496, *Av.* 1649. It is used of time in *Nub.* 496: and so here, 'in a trice.' Meineke reads χρόνου for χρόνῳ. *Nub.* 496 ἀκαρῆ (χρόνον) appears to support χρόνῳ here.

247. χαίρω κ.τ.λ.] 'I know when to hoard and when to spend.'

249. ἰδεῖν σε β.] 'I wish my wife and son to see you.' τὴν γ. and τὸν υἱὸν are subjects, σὲ object, to ἰδεῖν.

252. τί γάρ] Plutus had said, 'I believe you.' 'Why shouldn't you?' replies Chremylus, 'what reason could I have for deceiving you?' But Plutus of course means his belief to apply specially to μετὰ σέ: he can well believe that Chremylus puts his wife and son after riches.

253—321. Carion returns with the friends of Chremylus, whom he urges to make haste. As they are on their way he tells them that Chremylus has Plutus in his house, who is to make them all rich. They dance for joy, and exchange rude jests with Carion, as he leads them into Chremylus' presence.

253. ταὐτὸν θυμὸν φ.] 'Eaters of the same fare, and therefore snarers in his poverty.'

255. κ. οὐχὶ μέλλειν] 'It is not the time for any one to delay, but the very moment when one ought to be present and help.' The article, says Meineke, 'ferri non potest;' and he proposes μέλλει. But he quotes *Thesm.* 661 ὡς ὁ καιρός ἐστι μὴ μέλλειν ἔτι, which appears exactly the same.

261. οὔκουν κ.τ.λ.] 'I have been telling you all the while : your hard life is to be at an end.' 'How?' 'Why, Chremylus has got an old man.' 'With heaps of money of course.' 'Heaps of age and infirmity rather.' At which the Chorus are indignant, and they begin to quarrel ; but at last Carion tells them it is the god of wealth.

266. μαδῶντα] φαλακρόν, Schol. Probably the word suggested a more unsightly baldness than the common φαλακρός.

268. χρυσὸν ἐπῶν] 'gold of words,' i.e. words that are all gold, that imply golden wealth. They guess that from l. 262, and because such a wretched old fellow as Carion describes must have a heap of money.

270. μὲν οὖν] 'Nay, I haven't said anything yet about his money, only about his age and infirmities.'

273. πάντως γὰρ] He puts on the indignant surprise of injured innocence, at which the others laugh.

275. ὡς σεμνὸς] Cf. *Ran.* 178 ὡς σεμνὸς ὁ κατάρατος. 'You give yourself airs, but you're a rascal all the while.'

βοῶσιν] 'your shins cry aloud wanting the stocks and fetters.' They are said to feel the want of them because they are so used to them.

277. ἐν τῇ σορῷ κ.τ.λ.] Carion retorts on the leader of the Chorus that he ought to be dead, the coffin is his proper place. But reference is made to the Athenian custom of allotting different courts to different dicasts. These courts were distinguished by a particular letter : and a token or ticket (σύμβολον), and, as some say, a staff corresponding to his court, was given to each dicast. 'Whereas your letter shows that your allotted court is the coffin, yet you don't move thither, though Charon is ready to give you your ticket of admission.' λαχὸν τὸ γράμμα is an absolute case, and δὲ in σὺ δέ is superfluous in apodosis : whence Brunck proposes σύ γ'. One Scholiast thinks Χάρων is an anagram for ἄρχων 'the archon.'

279. μόθων] Cf. *Eq.* 632 κόβαλοι καὶ μόθων.

282. οἳ πολλὰ κ.τ.λ.] 'Who came, though hard-worked and busy, not even stopping to eat.' The Scholiast explains διεκπερῶντες 'overlooking and running past in our haste.' Also θύμοι as βολβοὶ 'onions' or ἀγριοκρόμμυα 'wild garlic.'

287. Μίδας] Μίδαις Meineke. The accusative may be defended in such constructions : but with πλουσίοις in the preceding line the dative is more natural. Porson and Dobree preferred πλουσίους in the line before.

290. καὶ μὴν κ.τ.λ.] Carion proposes to lead them dancing like the Cyclops: they, as his sheep, goats, and he-goats, are to follow.

θρεττανελὸ] Imitative of the cithara : cf. τήνελλα *Ach.* 1230, *Av.* 1764.

291. παρενσαλεύων] He gives a specimen of the kind of measure he means to dance.

292. τέκεα κ.τ.λ.] 'Come, children, repeatedly crying aloud and bleating like sheep and goats, follow my shepherding, and you he-goats shall get some breakfast.' They are hungry (cf. l. 282): so is he: cf. below, l. 320.

296. ἡμεῖς δέ γε] 'Then will we treat you as Ulysses and his crew did the Cyclops, and, while you are lying asleep after your drinking, will bore out your eye.' Cf. *Odyss.* ι. 371—390.

301. σφηκίσκον] The Scholiast recognizes this word, explaining it ὠξυμμένον ξύλον ἐπεὶ καὶ ὁ σφὴξ ὀξὺς ἐκ τῶν ὄπισθεν. Bentley would have read σφηνίσκον, which Meineke accepts. A pointed stake is meant in either case: it is a μόχλος in Homer.

316. ἀλλ' εἶα κ.τ.λ.] A truce to jest: we have more serious work in hand, for which I will try to prepare by getting a bit of something to eat.

321—414. The approach of the Chorus being told to Chremylus, he comes out to welcome them. They promise to help him. Meanwhile Blepsidemus has got some information about Chremylus' good fortune, and comes post haste to find out what is the truth. Being told that his friend is in a fair way to be wealthy, but at some risk, he at once concludes that he has stolen money, and wants to get some of it. In vain Chremylus asserts his honesty; till at last he tells him that he has found the god of wealth, and that he is going to get him cured of his blindness in Æsculapius' temple.

322. χαίρειν] The order is προσαγορεύειν μὲν ὑμᾶς χαίρειν ἀρχαῖόν ἐστιν, 'to bid you hail is old fashioned;' it is too common a form of greeting. For σαπρὸν cf. *Pac.* 554 εἰρήνης σαπρᾶς, where however it is an epithet of praise. Cf. also *Nub.* 984 ἀρχαῖα καὶ διπολιώδη.

325. συντεταμένως] A certain correction made by Bentley for συντεταγμένως. It satisfies the metre and is better for the sense. For κατεβλ. cf. *Av.* 1323 ὡς βλακικῶς διακονεῖς.

326. ὅπως] Supply ὁρᾶτε, as in numerous passages.

328. βλέπειν Ἄρη] βλέπειν with a noun is very common in Aristophanes: *Ach.* 566 etc. This very phrase is from Æschylus *Sept. c. Theb.* 53 λεόντων ὡς Ἄρη δεδορκότων.

330. ὡστιζόμεσθ'] Cf. *Ach.* 24 εἶτα δ' ὡστιοῦνται πῶς δοκεῖς ἐλθόντες ἀλλήλοισι περὶ πρώτου ξύλου.

331. παρείην] 2 aor. from παρίημι, 'I should allow any one to take Plutus himself from me.' The difference of mood in ὡστιζόμεσθα and παρείην is correct for the sense. 'It were a shame if we jostle (as we do) in the assembly and then I were to let Plutus slip from my hands.'

332. Βλεψίδημον] ὁ πρὸς τὸν δῆμον βλέπων καὶ ἐκ τούτου τὰ πρὸς ζωὴν ποριζόμενος. Schol.

338. κουρείοισι] Cf. *Av.* 1441. Barbers' shops have always been places for gossip.

341. χρηστόν τι πράττων] In prosperity it was unlike an Athenian to be ready to send for friends to share the good.

347. ἔσομαι μὲν οὖν] 'Nay I shall be, I am not so yet.' ἔνι= ἔνεστι.

350. ἦν μὲν κ.τ.λ.] The risk is 'perpetual prosperity if we succeed, utter annihilation if we fail.'

352. φορτίον] B. speaks as a merchant valuing a cargo : 'plainly this cargo is bad, I don't like it,' he suspects something unsound.

359. Ἄπολλον ἀπ.] Cf. *Av.* 61, *Vesp.* 161.

364. ὑγιαίνειν] As in *Nub.* 1275, *Av.* 1214, and below l. 1060.

365. ὡς πολύ] B. pathetically laments his friend's fall from the path of honesty: but of course is all the while looking to go shares with him.

367. κατὰ χώραν ἔ.] 'keeps its place, remains steady.'

368. ἐπίδηλόν τι πεπανουργηκότι] This must be rendered 'but it (the look) plainly belongs to one who has committed some rascality.' But πεπανουργηκότος would have been more natural. Bergk corrects τι πεπανουργηγχ' ὅτι, Meineke ὅτι πεπανούργηκέ τι, 'it is plain that he has committed some rascality.' Neither seems quite good enough to be certain : but the common text can hardly be right.

371. τὸ δ' ἐστίν] 'It is not as you think, but quite otherwise.' 'Not theft then, but open violence?' says B.

372. κακοδαιμονᾷς] Cf. Xen. *Mem.* 2. 1. 5, ἆρ' οὐκ ἤδη τοῦτο παντάπασι κακοδαιμονῶντός ἐστιν ; cf. below l. 501. The word is stronger than οὐχ ὑγιαίνειν and μελαγχολᾶν.

377. ἐγὼ κ.τ.λ.] B. at last proposes to hush up the matter, if paid for it.

379. ἐπιβύσας] Cf. *Pac.* 645 οἱ ξένοι χρυσίῳ τῶν ταῦτα ποιούντων ἐβύνουν τὸ στόμα.

380. φίλως γ'] 'Yes, a pretty friend you are ! you'd spend three minae and charge me twelve.'

382. ὁρῶ] B. with prophetic vision sees Chremylus impeached and suppliant, bringing wife and children to move the judges' pity, as the custom was. Cf. Dem. *c. Mid.* 574; also Aristoph. *Vesp.* 977 in the trial of the dog.

385. Ἡρακλειδῶν] There appears to have been a picture at Athens by Pamphilus of the Heracleidae as suppliants for aid from Athens against Eurystheus.

388. ἀπαρτί] From Herodot. II. 158 ἀπὸ τούτου εἰσὶ στάδιοι χίλιοι ἀπαρτὶ εἰς τὸν Ἀραβικὸν κόλπον, the meaning appears to be 'just, exactly.' And the Scholiast explains by ἀπηρτισμένως. L. and S. say it means here and in a fragment of Pherecrates ' just the reverse.' Surely

this is incorrect: here the whole sense is 'I am not a dishonest thief, as you suppose; it is just exactly the honest whom I am going to make rich.' And indeed Pherecrates may be explained in the same way. The words are A. τί σαυτὸν ἀποτίνειν τῷδ' ἀξιοῖς; B. ἀπαρτὶ δήπου προσλαβεῖν παρὰ τοῦδ' ἔγωγε μᾶλλον, 'What think you you ought to pay him?' 'Surely it is just I rather that should receive from him.'

390. ἀπολεῖς] με he was going to say, but B. breaks in.

396. Ποσειδῶ] Being asked to swear by Hestia, he swears by Poseidon (perhaps a greater oath): then he is asked whether he means the real genuine Poseidon of the sea, and replies that he means him and any other possible Poseidon too.

397. διαπέμπεις] 'send across' the wealth, or some of it: μεταδοῦναι in l. 400 shows this to be the meaning.

400. οὐ τῷ μ.] οὐκ ἔστιν ἐν τῷ μ. ' have not yet reached the distributing stage.' Some read τῳ.

402. ἑνί γέ τῳ τρόπῳ] Cf. *Thesm.* 430 ἢ φαρμάκοισιν ἢ μιᾷ γέ τῳ τέχνῃ, and below l. 413 ἕν γέ τι.

404. οὐκ ἐτός] 'he might well never come to me, that accounts then for his never coming to me.' Cf. *Ach.* 411 οὐκ ἐτὸς χωλοὺς ποιεῖς.

408. οὔτε γὰρ κ.τ.λ.] Doctors are not sufficiently paid now-a-days, and their art is degenerate.

409. οὐκ ἔστιν] sc. ἰατρός.

411. κατακλίνειν] The same method of cure was adopted unsuccessfully for Philocleon in *Vesp.* 124 νύκτωρ κατέκλινεν αὐτὸν εἰς Ἀσκληπιοῦ.

413. ἕν γέ τι] 'Make haste and do something.'

415—486. Poverty, having learnt what they are doing, bursts in indignant, with threats. At first she is jeered at: but when she names herself, Blepsidemus is terrified, and can hardly be persuaded to face her. Chremylus however is confident that with Wealth they can overcome her. He tells Poverty that they are doing no wrong to her, and are doing good to mankind. In this last they are, she tells them, mistaken: she, Poverty, is really a cause of good. This she offers to prove to their satisfaction: and the case is to be regularly argued.

415. ὦ θερμὸν κ.τ.λ.] Cf. Eur. *Med.* 1121 ὦ δεινὸν ἔργον παρανόμως εἰργασμένη. For θερμὸν 'rash' cf. Soph. *Trach.* 1046 ὦ πολλὰ δὴ καὶ θερμὰ μοχθήσας ἐγώ.

416. ἀνθρωπαρίῳ] A contemptuous diminutive.

419. τόλμημα κ.τ.λ.] A line of tragic sound and weight: hence Blepsidemus guesses her to be an Erinys.

421. ἀπολώλατον] The threat was ἐξολῶ: but the result is so certain that it is now looked on as completed.

424. γέ τοι] These particles give a proof or reason. So below in l. 1041, and elsewhere.

425. ἀλλ' οὐκ ἔχει γάρ] ' But no (she can't be that), for she has no torches.' ' Well then, she shall suffer for it,' says B.

426. πανδοκεύτριαν κ.τ.λ.] Women of this class seem to have been proverbial for noisy abuse. Cf. *Vesp.* 1388—1410: and *Ran.* 858 λοιδορεῖσθαι δ' οὐ θέμις ἄνδρας ποιητὰς ὥσπερ ἀρτοπώλιδας.

431. βάραθρον] To which constantly Aristophanes' characters consign what they hate. Cf. *Nub.* 1450, *Ran.* 574, etc.

433. ἥ] 'I am she who etc.'

435. καπηλίς] οἰνοπῶλις, Schol. The next line shows this, for she cheats him by short measure in the cup, or by mixing water with the wine.

443. ἐξωλέστερον] Active in sense: the word is generally passive.

447. ἀπολιπόντε ποι] The enclitic seems misplaced for the sense. Meineke inclines to read ἀπολιπόντες εἰ with ἐργασόμεθα τὸν θεὸν in the line before. If the text be retained, ποι must be connected with ἀπολιπόντε 'having gone away from him somewhither;' φευξούμεθα expressing the cowardly flight from poverty.

450. ποῖον κ.τ.λ.] Poverty makes us defenceless, our arms are pawned.

453. τροποῖον...τρόπων] There appears to be some intention of a play on the word, which is not worth reproducing in translation. The genitive is used of the person for whose defeat the trophy is raised. τῶν ταύτης τρόπων 'her bad ways.'

462. ἀνθρώποισιν ἐκπ.] Meineke would prefer to read ἀνθρώποις ἀγάθ' ἐκπ., and in the next line τί δ' ἄν ποθ' ὑμεῖς.

466. εἰ τοῦτο κ.τ.λ.] It would be a greater hurt to mankind if having once meant to drive out Poverty we were to forget to do it.

468. αὐτοῦ] Join with τούτου 'this very point.'

468—70. κἂν μὲν...εἰ δὲ μή] 'If I prove my case, well: if not punish me as you please.' This kind of ellipse is not uncommon. Cf. *Thesm.* 536, Hom. *Il. a.* 135.

476. ὦ τύμπανα κ.τ.λ.] This line and l. 478 are better given to Chremylus than to Blepsidemus. τύμπανον 'a cudgel:' the punishment of beating even to death with cudgels was in use. The verb occurs in the Epistle to the Hebrews xi. 35 ἄλλοι ἐτυμπανίσθησαν: and we read of Eleazar in 2 Macc. 6. 19 αὐθαιρέτως ἐπὶ τὸ τύμπανον προσῆγε. But some explain τύμπανον to be the frame to which the victims were bound. The κύφων appears to have been much the same as the κλῳός: cf. *Vesp.* 897.

480. τίμημ' ἐπιγρ.] The accuser set down the penalty which he thought was deserved. This might be set down differently by the other side, and was finally settled by the court. In the mock trial of the dog (*Vesp.* 894) the indictment concludes: τίμημα κλῳὸς σύκινος.

485. οὐκ ἂν φθάνοιτε] Cf. below l. 874 εἰς ἀγορὰν ἰὼν οὐκ ἂν φθάνοις and l. 1133 ἀποτρέχων οὐκ ἂν φθάνοις. The construction is also found in Herod. VII. 162 and in Plato. L. and S. explain it as a question 'Will you not be quick in doing?' Others as 'You cannot be too quick in doing.' Either way it means 'Make haste and do.'

487—618. Chremylus and Poverty argue out the case. Chremylus argues that the honest and good ought to be rich, but are not so: if Plutus had eyes, they would be so. Poverty says that want is the incentive to work: all trade and prosperity depends upon it: poverty is a hard teacher, but a good one: the thrifty poor may live contented: whereas wealth and luxury bring much evil and disease. Various arguments and examples are quoted. Chremylus will not be convinced; and Poverty, while protesting that they will want her back again, is compelled to depart.

488. μαλακὸν δ' ἐνδ.] Cf. Herod. III. 105 τὰς δὲ θηλέας (λέγουσι) ἐνδιδόναι μαλακὸν οὐδέν.

489. φανερὸν γνῶναι] 'plain to see,' *manifestum visu.* Cf. above, l. 49 δῆλον γνῶναι.

492. μόλις εὕρομεν κ.τ.λ.] The order is μόλις εὕρομεν βούλευμα ὥστε γενέσθαι τοῦτο, βούλευμα καλὸν καὶ γένναιον κ.τ.λ. 'We, desiring this to be so, with difficulty found a plan that it might be so.' The Scholiast and commentators discuss the difference between βούλευμα and βούλημα, words often confused and not widely different. In βούλευμα there is more of 'deliberation, reflection, inventiveness;' in βούλημα more of 'wish, intention.' Here βούλευμα seems preferable.

496. κᾷτα ποιήσει] If the good only are rich, the bad, seeing this, will give up their bad ways and become good, and then rich also.

499. οὔτις] The best MSS. have οὐδείς: Meineke reads οὐδέν, and τὶς in the preceding line. This does not seem good: οὐδέν is not a natural answer to any word in the foregoing question. No doubt οὐδείς is more forcible than οὔτις. By a transposition we might keep it οὐδείς· τούτου 'γώ σοι μάρτυς. A similar interruption of two disputants is in *Ran.* 1012, Α. τί παθεῖν φήσεις ἄξιος εἶναι; Δ. τεθνάναι· μὴ τοῦτον ἐρώτα. Holden reads τί ἂν ἐξεύροις and οὐδέν.

501. κακοδαιμονίαν] Even stronger than μανία: see above l. 372.

502. ὄντες] Join with πονηροί. But the separation by πλουτοῦσι is remarkable.

503. αὐτά] τὰ χρήματα implied in πλουτοῦσι. Meineke proposes hesitatingly αὐτόν, as had Hemsterhuys before him.

505. οὐκοῦν εἶναί φημ' εἰ κ.τ.λ.] 'Therefore I say that, if Plutus shall make an end of this deity (Poverty), there is a way by which one may go and provide greater blessings for men.' παύσει appears better than παῦσαι.

507. ἀλλ' ὦ κ.τ.λ.] 'You pair of easily gulled old fools, what you wish for will be the worst thing possible for you.' οὐχ ὑγιαίνειν as above, l. 364.

508. ξυνθιασώτα] 'A pretty pair of cronies in folly and craziness.'

511. τέχνην...σοφίαν] 'handicraft or profession.' Or, in the same art, σοφία may be the theory, the inventive part, τέχνη the practice, the manual part. Thus the Scholiast explains it : σοφία καλεῖ τὴν πανουργίαν καὶ μηχανήν, τέχνην δὲ τὴν μεταχείρησιν αὐτὴν καὶ ἐνέργειαν.

515. καρπὸν Δηοῦς θ.] Probably a quotation from some tragic writer.

521. ἔμπορος] 'Some merchant will sell us slaves, having got them out of Thessaly from the numerous kidnappers there.' Meineke adopts ἄπιστων : to which the Scholiast gives some countenance, telling us that the Thessalians were proverbially ἄπιστοι : though yet he seems to have read πλείστων.

ἀνδραποδιστῶν] In the Scholiasts here are given two explanations of ἀνδράποδον : ἀνδράποδον δὲ εἴρηται ὁ πούς ὁ ἐν τοῖς ἀνδράσιν ἀπὸ τοῦ ὑποκειμένου μέρους τῷ ὅλῳ· ὑπόκειται γὰρ ὁ οἰκέτης τῷ δεσπότῃ καθάπερ ὁ πούς τῷ ὅλῳ σώματι : and εἴρηται δὲ ἀνδραποδιστὴς παρὰ τὸ ἄνδρας ἀποδίδοσθαι, τούτεστι πωλεῖν. Neither derivation is quite satisfactory.

522. οὐδ' ἔσται] If there's no poverty, no one will run risks in order to get more money. The argument is not quite fair : for Chremylus was not going to do away with Poverty altogether, merely to banish her from himself and his honest friends.

526. ἐς κεφαλὴν σοί] Cf. *Pac.* 1063 I. ὦ μέλεοι θνητοὶ καὶ νήπιοι. T. ἐς κεφαλὴν σοί. Cf. *Ach.* 833 where τρέποιτο is added.

530. l. β. δαπάναις] 'with costly dyed garments.' ποικιλομόρφων the Scholiast explains by ἐγχρωμάτων which seems nearly the same as βαπτῶν. Perhaps it is rather 'broidered with various patterns' as a bride might naturally be in 'raiment of needlework.'

531. τί πλέον πλ. ἐστι] 'What advantage is it that one should be rich, if one has none of all these things?' Meineke reads ἔσται with Porson, ἀποροῦντι with Valkenaer. Both the present tense and the accusative case appear defensible; but ἔσται is a very slight change. The MSS. have ἀποροῦντα or ἀποροῦντας.

533. ἐπαναγκάζουσα] I compel men to work for their living : hence all invention and handicraft.

534. πενίαν] Meineke proposes πεῖναν, 'hunger :' but cf. l. 594.

535. ἐκ βαλανείου] The poor from want of sufficient clothing sought shelter from the cold in the baths : then exposure to the cold air raised these blisters. Schol.

536. κολοσυρτοῦ] Better than κολοσυρτόν : for a κολοσυρτὸς of blisters is strange language. πλὴν as preposition governs κολοσυρτοῦ as well as φῴδων, 'Except blisters and a posse of starving little ragamuffins and old crones.'

537. φθειρῶν κ.τ.λ.] Then there are the innumerable vermin and so forth, which trouble the beggar's rest. Join οὐδὲ λέγω ἀριθμὸν, 'And I cannot even recount the number etc.'

540. ἔχειν] This depends on πορίσαι δύναι' ἂν repeated, as do ἔχειν and σιτεῖσθαι in ll. 542, 3. The next few lines give a graphic list of all the cheap and mean accompaniments of poverty.

545. θράνου] Only used by Aristophanes in this place. From it comes θρανίτης (for which cf. Ach. 162) 'the rower on the topmost bench.' Homer has θρῆνυς for 'footstool.' The reading varies here between θράνου and θράνους.

546. φιδάκνης] Said to be specially Attic for πιθάκνης. In Eq. 792 however we have πιθάκναισι, and Meineke reads πιθάκνης here.

ἐρρωγυῖαν καὶ ταύτην] 'Broken too even this.' Several editors call this a 'rara trajectio' for καὶ ταύτην ἐρρωγυῖαν, and bring this passage and one from Plato's Rep. 341, to support their punctuation τὴν πόλιν καὶ ταῦτ' ἔχοντες in Ran. 703. See the note there. In this passage the arrangement of the words ἐρρ. κ. τ. appears perfectly natural : 'broken too this as well as the other.'

547. ἀγαθῶν] 'A nice lot of blessings I prove you to bestow on men, don't I?'

548. ὑπεκρούσω] ἐφθέγξω, ἀνεκρούσω, ἀπὸ μεταφορᾶς τῶν κιθαρῶν. Schol. 'It is not my life you have spoken of, but the life of beggars that you are harping on.' Such appears to be the sense. Of the middle voice ὑποκρούεσθαι I find no other instance. The active is used in Ar. Ach. 38 βοᾶν ὑποκρούειν 'to shout, to interrupt noisily.' But L. and S. refer to the Anthology for the meaning 'to accompany.' And the middle ἀνακρούεσθαι=ἀναβάλλεσθαι occurs Theocr. 4. 31 κᾖυ μὲν τὰ Γλαύκας ἀγκρούομαι. Meineke changes the reading here to ἐπεκρούσω on the authority of Pollux, who says that Aristophanes has used ἐπικρούεσθαι in the sense of νουθετῆσαι. But the only other uses of ἐπικρούειν are in the active : Thesm. 1004 ἐπικρ. ἧλον 'to hammer in a nail.' We may therefore acquiesce in ὑπεκρούσω here.

550. ὑμεῖς γ' κ.τ.λ.] 'Yes, you may think poverty and beggary own sisters, you who think Thrasybulus the tyrant-expeller and Dionysius the tyrant much the same.' A line which shows this to be the later Plutus.

551. ἀλλ' οὐχ οὑμὸς] My life is not so, nor ever will be : true poverty is thriftiness, diligence, without superfluities yet without wants.

555. ὡς μακαρίτην] A blessed life indeed the poor man's, who doesn't leave even enough to pay his funeral !

560. ἀσελγῶς] 'by riotous living :' the adverb expresses the way by which they come to be gouty etc.

561. σφηκώδεις] The wiry wasp-like character vexatious to foemen is well illustrated by the description which the old wasp chorus give of themselves in Vesp. 1072—83.

565. γοῦν] Ironical. 'A very orderly thing it is, for example, to steal!'

566. νὴ τὸν Δί'] Many editors reject this line: the metre wants mending, and the sense is obscure. Yet all the MSS. have it, and so had the Scholiast; his note is, 'In old times stealing was no disgrace if the thief was not found out.' None of the emendations proposed are satisfactory: the sense wanted is something like this: νὴ τὸν Δία γ' εἰ δὲ λαθὼν κλέπτῃ, πῶς οὐ τόδε κόσμιόν ἐστι; 'if the act is not seen, how does it offend against decorum?'

567. σκέψαι κ.τ.λ.] 'See how orators are honest while poor, but are corrupted by wealth.' The truth of this Chr. at once owns, but will not give up his main point.

572. κομήσῃς] Cf. above l. 170. Connect together κλαύσει ὁτιὴ ζητεῖς: μηδὲν—κομήσῃς is parenthetical.

575. πτερυγίζεις] 'You flap and flutter' with plenty of show and noise but no argument. Met. from young birds: or from a cock crowing.

καὶ πῶς] Chremylus thinks that now he has got an argument: 'If you, Poverty, are better than Wealth, how is it that all men fly from you?' 'They don't like being improved.'

578. χαλεπὸν πρᾶγμ'] 'So difficult is it to see what is right.' 'Then Zeus doesn't see what is best,' urges Chr., 'for he is rich.' 'No he is not,' replies Poverty.

581. Κρονικαῖς λήμαις] Cronos had become a proverb for all that was old-world, out of date, 'ante-diluvian' as we might say. Cf. *Nub.* 398 Κρονίων ὄζων, 929 Κρόνος ὤν, 1070 Κρόνιππος. Also Plat. *Lys.* 205 C, ἃ ἡ πόλις ᾄδει περὶ τῶν προγόνων, ταῦτα ποιεῖ τε καὶ λέγει, πρὸς δὲ τούτοις ἔτι τούτων κρονικώτερα. For λημᾶν cf. *Nub.* 327, εἰ μὴ λημᾷς κολοκύνταις.

584. ἵνα κ.τ.λ.] 'Where, in which.' The Olympic games were celebrated at intervals of four years. Pindar (*Ol.* III. 38) calls the festival πενταετηρὶς by inclusive reckoning, as here we have δι' ἔτους πέμπτου.

586. κοτίνῳ] From adj. κοτινοῦς: Porson's reading. κοτίνῳ would be subst. in apposition. κοτίνου some old editions had, but the MS. authority supports the dative.

587. οὐκοῦν κ.τ.λ.] It is not from lack of gold that Zeus gives the wild olive wreath, but from miserly stinginess.

589. λήροις] 'trumpery, valueless trifles.'

ἑᾷ] κεῖσθαι the Scholiast supplies. Zeus leaves it untouched in his coffers, spares to take of it.

590. περιάψαι] Cf. *Ach.* 640 τιμὴν περιάψας. Plato uses αἰσχύνην περιάπτειν, Xenophon ἀνελευθερίαν π., which is exactly the quality mentioned in l. 591.

592. ἀλλὰ σέ γ᾽ ὁ Ζεύς] This is abuse, not argument. Chremylus seems to mean ' May you get nothing better than the olive crown ! you'll find it a barren honour.' Cratinus is described in *Eq.* 534 as going about στέφανον μὲν ἔχων αὖον δίψῃ δ᾽ ἀπολωλώς. But the Scholiast says there is a double meaning in the phrase : whence one commentator supposes that κοτίνῳ στ. στεφανῶσαι might mean ' to beat the head with a club of olive-wood.'

593. τὸ γὰρ τολμᾶν] 'To think that you should dare !' Cf. *Nub.* 268, *Ran.* 741.

594. Ἑκάτης] On the first day of the month the wealthy set out at the crossways a meal for Hecate: this the poor and starving took. Chremylus' argument is : The rich have enough and to spare : the poor are forced to starve or steal : Hecate's offerings prove this.

600. οὐ γὰρ πείσεις] ' A man convinced against his will is of the same opinion still.'

601. ὦ πόλις Ἄργους] This line occurs in *Eq.* 813 : the first half is said to be from Euripides' *Telephus*, the last is found in *Medea* 168.

602. Παύσωνα] Pauson was a painter : in *Ach.* 854 called παμπόνηρος, in *Thesm.* 949 spoken of as poor and starving. Chremylus bids Poverty call Pauson, her messmate, and get his help and companionship, but leave himself (Chremylus), and not come back till sent for.

612. σέ...κεφαλήν] τὴν κεφαλὴν appears to be in a kind of apposition to σέ. ' It is best for me to enjoy my wealth, and, as for you, to let your head (=you) go weep.' The same phrase occurs with a dative in *Vesp.* 584 κλάειν ἡμεῖς μακρὰ τὴν κεφαλὴν εἰπόντες τῇ διαθήκῃ. The head, as the noblest part or the part chiefly affected, stands for the whole person in such phrases as γένναιον, δύστηνον κάρα, ἐς κεφαλὴν σοι : compare Lat. ' multa fleturum caput.' In this passage κεφαλὴν can hardly be (as Bergler takes it) accus. of object to κλάειν.

619—626. Being now rid of Poverty Chremylus carries out his plan. Plutus is taken to Asclepius' temple. After l. 626 the choral ode is lost, which should have entertained the audience during the performance of the cure which Carion reports.

619. ἡμῖν] Join with οἴχεται : ' we have got rid of this plaguy creature.'

623. τῶν προὔργου] ' the needful things,' i.e. the taking Plutus to the temple.

624. στρώματα] For Plutus to lie on. In the *Frogs* Xanthias carries στρώματα for Dionysus in his journey to the nether world.

627—770. Carion returns with good news to the rejoicing Chorus and to Chremylus' wife, whom their cries of joy attract. They require a full account. He relates in amusing style how they lay down to rest in the temple : how the priest made booty of the offerings ; how he and an old woman did the same; how finally Asclepius went his round among the patients, and treated an impostor as he deserved, but restored Plutus to sight. Plutus, he says, with a crowd of followers will soon be there.

627. ὦ πλεῖστα κ.τ.λ.] 'Ye who have sopped up most broth with least meal.' For the μυστίλη, a kind of spoon made of bread, cf. *Eq.* 1168, where the perf. part. of the verb is used, but rather differently. Cf. also *Eq.* 827 ἀμφοῖν χεροῖν μυστιλᾶται τῶν δημοσίων. For the use of ἐπί cf. *Ach.* 855, *Eq.* 707, *Pac.* 123. The gist of Carion's address is : 'You who have had scanty fare and been glad to get a full meal at the Thesea are now coming in for a good time.'

631. τῶν σαυτοῦ φίλων] Added unexpectedly, to qualify the common term of address ὦ βέλτιστε : 'best of your own friends and fellow-slaves.' τῶν ὁμοίων σοι μαστιγιῶν Schol.

635. ἐξωμμάτωται κ.τ.λ.] Said by the Scholiast to be from the *Phineus* of Sophocles. Certainly the two lines have a tragic sound. The active ἐξομματοῦν is used in Aesch. *Prom. Vinct.* 506 φλογωπὰ σήματα ἐξωμμάτωσα πρόσθεν ὄντ' ἐπάργεμα.

637. χαρὰν...βοάν] Cause for joy, cause for shouting. These lines are rather in tragic style.

639. εὔπαιδα] Podalirius, Machaon, Panacea, and others, were the children of Asclepius; and all were skilful in their father's art. See below, l. 730.

643. τουτονί] Carion.

645. καὐτὴ] 'Yourself too' as well as I. Carion is to have a cup for his good tidings : and, as an inducement to the good wife to bring it, he tells her that she will have a share. He adds, perhaps as an aside, 'It is your pet weakness.' No other instance of φιλεῖν with participle is adduced : but στέργειν is so used. Meineke quotes from *Eccl.* 502 μίσει σάκον πρὸς τοῖν γναθοῖν ἔχουσα.

647. ποῦ 'στιν;] τὰ ἀγαθά. 'You will soon know them when I tell the tale.' Meineke punctuates after λεγομένοις : 'They are in what I have to tell.'

650. ἐκ τῶν ποδῶν] He simply means 'from beginning to end :' but the woman catching the words ἐς τὴν κεφαλήν σοι, which were often an imprecation 'on your head be the evil,' says 'Pray heaven it be not on *my* head !' 'What ! do you pray that the *blessings* may not be on your head ?' says Carion. 'No I mean the *troubles*,' replies she, having understood πράγματα in that sense.

653. ὡς γὰρ κ.τ.λ.] Carion tells his tale like a messenger in a tragedy.

657. ἐλοῦμεν] Contr. from ἐλόομεν, as λούμενος from λοόμενος. Cf. *Nub.* 1044 λοῦσθαι and 838 καταλόει. L. and S. say that in these forms 'the Attics omit the vowel of inflexion.' Rather, as καταλόει shows, the υ of the long stem is omitted. This υ probably represents an original digamma : compare the Latin *lavo*, and such Homeric forms as λοεσσάμενος, λοετρὰ point to λο as the verbal stem.

εὐδαίμων ἄρ'] This is said with a touch of pity and doubt whether the cold water cure was for the old man's happiness.

661. πέλανος] It is impossible to translate this otherwise than by making πέλανος an explanation of πόπανα καὶ προθύματα. But, though often used of a sacrificial offering, πέλανος does not suit well if thus taken. π. καὶ πρ. cannot reasonably be called 'a moist or clotted mixture,' which seems the meaning of πέλανος. Bergk proposes μέλανος: which Meineke thinks probable. Possibly a line has been lost, which gave another verb to πόπανα καὶ πρ., and a conjunction to καθωσιώθη πέλανος. Against relinquishing the word πέλανος there is its frequent sacrificial use: e. g. Eur. *Ion,* 706 καλλίφλογα πέλανον ἐπὶ πυρὶ καθαγνίσας. Cf. Aesch. *Ag.* 96, *Pers.* 204. And the whole line reads like a quotation from a tragedy, as indeed Holden prints it.

663. παρεκαττύετο] Properly καττύεσθαι is of shoe-maker's stitching. Cf. *Eq.* 314 οἶδ' ἐγὼ τὸ πρᾶγμ' ὅθεν καττύεται, in the mouth of Cleon the tanner. Here it is of heaping up the materials for a στιβάς.

665. Νεοκλείδης] Called Νεοκλείδης ὁ γλάμων in *Eccl.* 254, 398. The Scholiast says he was an orator.

666. ὑπερηκόντικεν] Cf. *Eq.* 659 διακοσίαισι βουσὶν ὑπερηκόντισα, and *Av.* 363.

669. παρήγγειλ' ἐγκ.] Porson's correction for παρήγγειλεν καθ.

673. ἀθάρης] The porridge was brought as an offering by the old woman, being (says the Scholiast) the food which toothless old women usually eat. ἐξέπληττε 'scared me,' i. e. kept me awake.

677. φθοῖς] acc. pl. contracted from φθόϊας, as οἶς from ὄϊας in Attic dialect.

679. περιῆλθε] So in the History of Bel we read that 'in the night came the priests, as they were wont to do, and did eat and drink up all' of the offerings made to the idol.

681. ἤγιζεν] Ironically said of the priestly theft, in which he pretends to see πολλὴν ὁσίαν 'great holiness.' If it was right in the priest to take the cakes, so was it right (he argues) for him to take the porridge.

685. νὴ τοὺς θεούς] 'Yes, I feared that the god would come, garlands and all, and eat the porridge.' Asclepius was represented on coins as wearing a chaplet of laurel.

687. ὁ γὰρ ἱερεύς] 'His priest had given me a lesson' to make the best of my time and get all I could.

689. τὴν χεῖρ' ὑφήρει] Meineke, from Dobree, adopts ἄρασ' ὑφῄρει. The Scholiast says ἐκτείνει κατὰ τῆς χύτρας ἵνα μηδεὶς αὐτὴν λάβῃ. Plainly the old woman made some attempt to save the porridge: upon which Carion bit her hand, frightened her, and got the porridge. But ὑφῄρει τὴν χεῖρα can hardly mean this: we want a word meaning 'she advanced' to contrast with πάλιν ἀνέσπασεν in l. 691. Holden, reading

ἄρασ', explains it 'raising her hand:' supplying τὴν χεῖρα, which has wrongly crept from a marginal note into the text.

690. παρείας] These snakes were sacred to Asclepius, and kept in his temple. Their bite was not dangerous. Demosthenes mentions them *De Corona* 313, τοὺς ὄφεις τοὺς παρείας θλίβων καὶ ὑπὲρ τῆς κεφαλῆς αἰωρῶν. The name παρείας was given them from the puffed shape of their heads probably. But the word is also written ταρώας, and L. and S. take it to be from their reddish-brown colour.

694. ἔφλων] Cf. *Pac.* 1306 φλᾶν ταῦτα πάντα καὶ σποδεῖν.

708. ἐκεῖνος] Asclepius.

712. λίθινον;] The wife begins to distrust Carion's veracity, and points out the absurdity of a κιβώτιον of stone: then again, how could Carion see all this, if he was wrapped up? But the slave is equal to the occasion: his doublet has loop-holes to spy through.

716. φάρμακον κ.] 'A plaster or poultice.' φάρμακα are distinguished as καταπλαστά, χριστά, ποτά, βρώσιμα. Aeschylus in *Prom. Vinct.* 480 speaks of three kinds: οὐκ ἦν ἀλέξημ' οὐδὲν, οὔτε βρώσιμον, οὐ χριστὸν, οὔτε πιστόν. Also ἐπιπαστὰ φάρμακα were used: Homer's leech treats a wound ἐπ' ἤπια φάρμακα πάσσων. Of the κατάπλασμα or ἔμπλαστρον this passage of Aristophanes gives a good description. The solids are pounded (τρίβειν, ἔφλα) then liquids are added to dilute it (διέμενος).

718. Τηνίων] Tenos was one of the Cyclades, noted for serpents and garlic.

719. ὀπὸν καὶ σχῖνον] Both, as the Scholiast says, δηκτικά: as also is the Sphettian vinegar. Sphettus was a deme of Attica. Either sharp vinegar was made there, or the people were πικροί, as one Scholiast tells us.

720. διέμενος] From δίημι: perhaps the only classical instance of its use in this meaning.

724. καταπεπλασμένος] 'Plastered over, with your plaster on.' Neocleides is bidden in *Eccl.* 404 to anoint his eyes with garlic and fig-juice.

725. ὑπομνύμενον] In Attic law ὑπόμνυσθαι was 'to swear that there was a cause for non-attendance,' such as illness. 'I will make you stay away from the assembly, putting in an affidavit of the reason, namely, illness.' This seems the meaning with τῆς ἐκκλησίας. But the Scholiast read ταῖς ἐκκλησίαις 'at the assemblies:' then the participle ὑπομνύμενον must be taken with παύσω 'I will stop you from hindering business by putting in false pleas, from being an obstructive.' ἐπομνύμενον was the old MS. reading. This one Scholiast explains ἐφεδρεύοντα καὶ συκοφαντοῦντα ὑπὲρ τοῦ κερδαίνειν. But others appear to be explaining ὑπομνύμενον. In any case Asclepius seems to mean that he will stop Neocleides deluding the assembly by false allegations or excuses, giving him, for once, a real reason to stay away.

727. Πλούτωνι] Though Πλούτων and Πλοῦτος be connected etymologically, yet the use of Πλούτωνι for Πλούτῳ here has no apparent reason. It is thought by some to be a diminutive of endearment, as γλίσχρων from γλίσχρος. Meineke proposes Πλούτῳ 'τι, that is Πλούτῳ ἔτι, 'he further went and sat by Plutus.' This has an awkward sound. Holden proposes Πλούτῳ γε. The particle γε appears at least useless.

729. ἡμιτύβιον] Said to be an Egyptian word. The first part looks like Greek ; but the Greeks when adopting a foreign word would write and modify it to suit their own language. Hippocrates uses it: it seems therefore a medical word : and Egyptian physicians were renowned in ancient times.

730. Πανάκεια] Daughter of the god. Cf. l. 639.

733. δράκοντ'] Serpents were everywhere associated with the worship of Aesculapius : he was transferred from Epidaurus to Rome, as the legend runs, in the form of a serpent.

ἐκ τοῦ νεὼ] The patients were within the τέμενος (l. 659) but not in the actual νεώς.

736. περιέλειχον] According to the legend serpents in the same way purged the ears of Cassandra and Helenus, that they might understand divine sounds and be able to prophesy. There is perhaps a special fitness in the ministration of serpents to heal the sight, as their name (δράκων) denotes keenness of sight. This the Scholiast notices here ; giving also as a reason for their attendance on the god of healing, that they renew their youth by casting their skin, and removal of disease is a kind of restoration of youth.

737. πρίν σε κ.τ.λ.] The measure of time is ludicrously adapted to the bibacity of the woman : for which see above l. 645.

742. πῶς δοκεῖς] Cf. note on *Nub.* 881. It must be connected with ἠσπάζοντο.

746. ὅτι βλ.] The ι is scanned long before βλ, which is according to rule. Bentley however proposed ὁτιὴ here.

750. ὑπερφυὴς ὅσος] A very common combination of adj. and relative ; as also is ὑπερφυῶς ὡς.

751—56. οἱ γάρ...ἅμα] The honest men are all glad, the rogues are sad and sorry.

757. οἱ δ'] That is οἱ δίκαιοι.

758. ἐκτυπεῖτο κ.τ.λ.] Mock-tragic in style. For κτυπεῖσθαι in place of the usual κτυπεῖν cf. *Thesm.* 995 ἀμφὶ δὲ σοὶ κτυπεῖται Κιθαιρώνιος ἠχώ. In the same play l. 121, 985 εὔρυθμος is used as epithet to κρούματα, πούς.

760. ἐξ ἑνὸς λόγου] 'Beginning at one word of command, at once, with one accord.'

764. ἀναδῆσαι εὐαγγέλια] Cf. *Eq.* 647 εἶτ' ἐστεφάνουν μ' εὐαγγέλια.

765. κριβανωτῶν] Some would read κριβανιτῶν, as in *Ach.* 87, 1123 κριβανίτης is the form used.

768. καταχύσματα] Nuts, figs, etc. were showered by way of welcome on a bride entering her home, or on a newly bought slave. Cf. Demosth. 1123, ἣ τὰ καταχύσματα αὐτοῦ κατέχεε τόθ' ἡνίκ' ἐωνήθη. The wife says that they must welcome Plutus' newly acquired eyes with a shower of bonbons.

771—801. A κομμάτιον or short stanza of the Chorus is wanting. Plutus comes in, ashamed of his former blindness, and determined to make up for it now by enriching good men. Chremylus follows, annoyed at the crowds that press on him now that he is prosperous. Then Plutus is welcomed by Chremylus' wife and they enter the house.

771. καὶ προσκυνῶ γε] Plutus' first words are a continuation or answer to something which has gone before : as the particles καὶ...γε show. Meineke thinks something has been lost. Holden thinks them a quotation.

775. οἴοις κ.τ.λ.] Explanatory of συμφοράς : 'I am ashamed of my wretched state, ashamed, that is, to think what rogues I consorted with and knew it not.'

778. ἐκεῖν'] The being with rogues. ταῦτα the shunning honest men.

779. πάλιν ἀναστ.] 'having just reversed all this.'

781. ἐνεδίδουν] Meineke reads ἐπεδίδουν. Cf. *Thesm.* 213 ἄγε νυν ἐπειδὴ σαυτὸν ἐπιδίδως ἐμοί. L. and S. refer to Eur. *Tro.* 687 ἐνδόντες τύχῃ παρεῖσαν αὑτοὺς κυμάτων δρομήμασιν, but αὑτοὺς there is governed by παρεῖσαν rather than by ἐνδόντες. Either compound seems defensible, and the MS. authority rather for ἐνεδίδουν.

782. βάλλ' ἐς κ.] To the troublesome crowd, or to one of them. Such an exclamation might do for many as well as for one. Cf. *Eq.* 634 ἄγε δὴ, Σκίταλοι.

783. οἱ φαινόμενοι] This is quite satisfactory. ὀσφραινόμενοι the conjecture of Hemsterhuys is neat but needless. The article with the participle is wanted ; and 'the friends that turn up, are visible' is excellent sense.

784. νύττουσι καὶ φλῶσι] 'poke and bruise my shins' by crowding round me. Some explain φλῶσι of touching the knees in supplication : but νύττουσι cannot mean that, and the two verbs with one accusative ἀντικνήμια must be of similar meaning.

787. περιεστεφάνωσεν] Not ἐτίμησεν, as Schol. explains ; but simply 'surrounded.'

788. ὦ φίλτατ'] Chremylus' wife returns, according to promise, with the bonbons. καὶ σὺ καὶ σὺ to Plutus and Chremylus.

790. μηδαμῶς] Plutus declines, because it would be unfitting to celebrate the entry of wealth by emptying the house of anything.

792. βλέψαντος] 'having become able to see, having got back my sight.' A similar use of the aorist is ἐπειδὴ Θησεὺς ἐβασίλευσεν, 'when Theseus became king,' Thuc. II. 15.

796. ἔπειτα κ.τ.λ.] 'Then too we shall escape the charge of vulgarity. For it ill beseems a dramatic poet to raise a laugh by a scramble among the audience for nuts and figs.' In *Vesp.* 58 Aristophanes disclaims such devices : ἡμῖν γὰρ οὐκ ἔστ' οὔτε κάρυ' ἐκ φορμίδος δούλῳ διαρριπτοῦντε τοῖς θεωμένοις. For the use of φόρτον cf. *Pac.* 748, τοιαῦτ' ἀφελὼν κακὰ καὶ φόρτον.

800. Δεξίνικος] Plainly he was some poor man who was standing up eager for the expected scramble.

802—957. Carion comes out and gives an amusing description of the new wealth of his master. An honest man, who is prosperous now but was poor before, comes to thank Plutus, and to hang up his old garments as a memorial. While he and Carion talk together, an informer enters, whose trade is spoilt. He and his complaints and threats are mocked at : they strip him of his clothes, put on him the old rags of the honest man, and send him away to the bath-house.

803. μηδὲν ἐξ.] At no expense, no outlay.

805. ἐπεισπέπαικεν] Said by the Scholiast to be a military term used of an invader. εἰσπαίειν is used by Sophocles, *O. T.* 1252 βοῶν γὰρ εἰσέπαισεν Οἰδίπους. The influx of good things is put comically as a riotous invasion which they have not deserved (οὐδὲν ἠδικηκόσιν): at the same time this last is a sarcasm on the usual mode of acquiring wealth at Athens : ὡς τῶν πολλῶν, μάλιστα τῶν Ἀθηναίων, ἐξ ἀδικίας πλουτούντων.

806. οὕτω τὸ πλ.] 'In this way to get rich is sweet.' There's a peculiar pleasure in wealth obtained thus. This line looks like an alternative for l. 802.

807. ἀνθοσμίου] Cf. *Ran.* 1150 Διόνυσε, πίνεις οἶνον οὐκ ἀνθοσμίαν.

810. φρέαρ] Some vessel for oil, not literally 'a well or spring.'

813. σαπροὺς] Meineke would change here, as elsewhere, to σαθρούς. In meaning the distinction commonly observed is that σαθρὸς is 'mouldering, crumbling to pieces from decay,' of rotten wood, ships, garments, etc.; σαπρὸς, 'rancid, sour, putrid,' of flesh, fish, etc. But the two qualities may co-exist in the same thing : and the words are etymologically akin. And the verb is used in both senses. Hence it appears safest to follow the MSS. Cf. above l. 542 σαπρὸς φορμός.

815. ἰπνὸς] Whether 'oven' here, or 'lantern,' as in *Pac.* 841, is doubtful.

ἀρτιάζομεν] The game which Horace (*Sat.* II. 3. 248) calls 'ludere par impar.' The Scholiast tells us that it was also called ζυγὰ ἢ ἄζυγα. Guessing whether the number of coins held up was odd or even was the point of the game.

820. ὗν κ.τ.λ.] A triple sacrifice appears to have been the right thing. It was called τριττύς. The Latins had the name 'suovetaurilia' for a sacrifice of pig, sheep, and bull. The combination of βουθυτεῖν with the other words may be compared with *Av.* 1232, μηλοσφαγεῖν τε βουθύτοις ἐπ᾽ ἐσχάραις.

822. ἔδακνε] Cf. *Ach.* 18 ἐδήχθην ὑπὸ κονίας τὰς ὀφρῦς.

823. παιδάριον] A slave is carrying his old doublet : cf. l. 842.

826. δῆλον ὅτι κ.τ.λ.] Holden punctuates with a full stop after δῆλον ὅτι: to avoid δῆλον ὅτι being followed by the weaker ὡς ἔοικας in one sentence. His reading will be ''Tis plain you are that (prosperous). You are, methinks, one of the honest.' And Meineke says these two δῆλον ὅτι and ὡς ἔοικας, 'adversis frontibus sibi repugnant.' This is questionable. ἔοικας need not really imply doubt, and may well enough go with δῆλον ὅτι. 'Nimirum, ut videtur' Brunck renders it. The personal construction of ἔοικας is common.

830. ἐπήρκουν] I helped my friends in need, thinking that this would be repaid to me should I be in need.

837. οἱ δ᾽ ἐξετρέποντο] Lucian, in his *Timon*, represents Timon as finding the same ingratitude : οἱ δὲ πόρρωθεν ἰδόντες ἑτέραν ἐκτρέπονται.

κοὐκ ἐδόκουν] Cf. *Pac.* 1051 μὴ νῦν ὁρᾶν δοκῶμεν αὐτόν.

839. αὐχμὸς γὰρ ὢν τ. σκ.] 'A drought that there was in your vessels.' Your vessels were no longer well supplied : your table no longer wealthy : hence your friends deserted you.

840. οὐχὶ νῦν] ἀπόλλυσί με αὐχμός. I am not now poor : and therefore in return for my prosperity (ἀνθ᾽ ὧν) I come to give thanks to the god Plutus.

842. θεῶν] Plainly this, the MS. reading, is right. Brunck rashly accepts πρὸς τὸν θεόν. The exclamation 'in the name of the gods!' is perfectly natural : the proposed correction is doubtful Greek.

845. μῶν ἐνεμυήθης κ.τ.λ.] The initiated wore the garments of their initiation till they fell to pieces : then dedicated them to some god. To the ragged garments at the Eleusinia there is allusion probably in *Ran.* 404. With μεγάλα understand μυστήρια. Notice that the ἐν in the compound verb has its force, 'were you initiated in it,' i.e. 'wearing it.'

847. συνεχειμάζετο] Shoes as well as coat have been old friends through cold and storm.

849. χαρίεντά γ᾽] Said with irony 'Very pretty gifts these!'

850. δείλαιος] The penultima is scanned short, as in *Nub.* 1474 οἴμοι δείλαιος.

853. συγκέκραμαι] Cf. Soph. *Ant.* 1311, δειλαίᾳ δὲ συγκέκραμαι δύᾳ. The Scholiast thinks the metaphor is from wine. And πολυφόρος is explained as 'strong,' πολυφόρος οἶνος being wine that will bear much admixture of water : for which idea cf. *Eq.* 1188 ὡς ἡδύς, ὦ Ζεῦ,

καὶ τὰ τρία φέρων καλῶς. Even if this be the right explanation of
πολυφόρος, yet to press the metaphor in συγκέκραμαι would make the
sufferer to be the water mixed with (and weakening) his own calamity.
If Aristophanes meant this, he meant the whole phrase to be in
ridicule of his tragic contemporaries. It is not likely that Sophocles
and Aeschylus meant κέκρασθαι δύᾳ, οἴκτῳ otherwise than 'to be
plunged in.' And πολυφόρῳ is also explained πολλὰ κακὰ φέροντι.
Of land it means 'fruitful, bearing much good:' therefore why not of
a fortune ' bearing much evil'?

856—9. οὐ γὰρ κ.τ.λ.] Am I not shamefully treated, who have
lost everything by Plutus' recovery of sight? Meineke doubts the correctness of πράγματα πέπονθα, and would prefer χρήματα, to be taken
with ἀπολωλεκώς.

859. αἱ δίκαι] The informer means to have 'legal' redress. Carion
now knows at once the stamp of the man : it is a bad coinage.

863. καλῶς ποιῶν ἀπ.] ' He does quite right in being ruined; it is
quite right he should be ruined.' Generally γε is added in this phrase,
as in *Pac.* 271 εὖ γε...ποιῶν ἀπόλωλ' ἐκεῖνος. And it is a sort of polite
thanks 'Very kind of him to do so.'

865. ὑποσχόμενος] Plutus was to make rich all the *good* men. The
informer reckons himself among the good.

868. τίνα] 'Whom has he harmed'? 'Why me.' 'Were you then
a rogue?' 'No, it's you that are the dishonest rogues: and no doubt
you've got my money.'

870. οὐ μὲν οὖν κ.τ.λ.] 'Nay rather there is no honesty in any one
of you.' ὑμῶν, which is emphatic, depends on οὐδενός, which is masc.
and not adverbial, either here or in l. 362 (as some commentators say),
but a possessive genitive, 'belonging to any one of you.'

872. σοβαρὸς] ἐπηρμένος καὶ μέγα φρονῶν. Schol. In Aristophanes
this adjective is generally with a verb of 'going, moving:' as *Ach.* 672
σοβαρὸν ἐλθὲ, *Nub.* 406 φέρεται σοβαρός, *Pac.* 83 σοβαρῶς χώρει.

874. οὐκ ἂν φθάνοις] See note on l. 485.

876. οἰμώξἄρα] οἰμώξει ἄρα. Cf. *Pac.* 532 κλαυσἄρα σύ.

881. ἐπεὶ κ.τ.λ.] He answers his own question, 'Yes, you are an
accomplice : for whence else this coat?'

884. δακτύλιον] A magic ring that can avert danger or illness. In
Athenaeus is a fragment of Antiphanes, where a man says that if he
has a pain παρὰ Φερτάτου δακτύλιός ἐστί μοι δραχμῆς. Eudamus and
Phertatus were persons who sold such charms.

885. ἀλλ' οὐκ ἔνεστι] The sense is plain, 'Your ring is of no avail
against an informer's bite:' but the Greek, as it stands, is not complete.
Dobree thinks one or more lines have been lost. ἀλλ' οὐ περίεσται, ἀλλ'
οὐκ ἀνέξει are conjectures. Holden suggests ἐπῳδὴ or ἴασις for ἔνεστι,
which may have been a marginal note. Or, as one Scholiast tells us

that δήγματος is the genitive after δακτύλιος understood. Holden supposes οὐ γὰρ ἐστὶ to have been his reading: 'the ring is not a ring of an informer's bite:' i.e. 'a ring valid against an informer's bite.'

889. τῷ γε σῷ] 'You are after no good.' 'No good to you certainly.'

890. δειπνήσετον] The savoury smell of Chremylus' preparations within reaches him. He maintains still that is at his cost they will feed.

891. ὡς δὴ 'π' ἀληθείᾳ] 'Utinam haec vera sint, tuque prae inedia disrumparis.' Meineke ἐπ' ἀληθείᾳ τῶν σοι λελεγμένων 'on condition of the truth of your words.' This seems the right explanation of ἐπ' ἀληθείᾳ. But the informer has just said they were going to feast at his cost ; therefore the whole sense must be : 'I wish we were going to do so, and that you and your witness might burst, not with eating indeed, but with spite and envy at seeing us eat while you get nothing.' And as διαῤῥαγείης might naturally first suggest a literal bursting from overeating, the last words are added as an after-thought. The whole answer is equivalent to an angry denial: hence in the next line ἀρνεῖσθον.

894. χρῆμα τεμαχῶν] Cf. *Ach.* 150 τὸ χρῆμα παρνόπων : also *Nub.* 2, *Eq.* 1219.

895. ὖ ὖ] ὀσφραινόμενος τοῦτό φησι. Schol.

896. ὀσφραίνει τι] The regular case after ὀσφρ., a verb of sense, is the genitive, as in τοῦ ψύχους. But a neuter accus. such as τι can follow any verb, being rather acc. of respect 'at all' than strictly the object of the ὄσφρησις.

897. ἀμπέχεται τ.] The informer is in wretched plight, wearing a threadbare coat. They strip him afterwards and give him one that is even worse. But what necessity is there for altering the text violently to ἀμφέξεται or ἀμφιεῖ, as De Velsen and Meineke propose to do?

903. γεωργὸς] A husbandman would, in the just man's estimation, be probably χρηστός. But the informer is not such a mad fool as to follow this profitless trade.

904. σκήπτομαι γ'] Merchants had certain exemptions from service and taxes. Hence it would pay to pretend that trade. Demosth. *c. Apaturium* 893 speaks of the dishonest use made of these privileges by pretended merchants, ἐπὶ τῇ προφάσει τοῦ ἐμπορεύεσθαι συκοφαντοῦντας.

ὅταν τύχω] Meineke denies that this can mean anything suitable, and would read ὅταν τύχῃ 'when it chance to be needful, when occasion requires.' The Scholiast's ὅταν γένηται καιρὸς πολέμου may seem to support this change. But the Greeks do use a personal construction where we prefer an impersonal: as ὡς ἔοικας, ὡς δοκεῖς (see above l. 826), 'as it seems likely.' And if 'when it so happen'='when occasion happen to need it,' why should not 'when I so happen'='when I happen to need it '?

906. μηδὲν π.] 'If you did nothing:' the negative μὴ with participle is conditional.

908. τί μαθών;] Cf. *Nub.* 1507 and 340, and the notes there. The answer βούλομαι refers to the Athenian principle that any one who wished (ὁ βουλόμενος) might bring a charge, make a speech, propose a measure. This is made clear below at l. 918.

910. σοὶ πρ. μηδέν] 'when it does not concern you.' προσῆκον is abs. like ἐξόν, παρόν. As the σοὶ in sense belongs to προσῆκον, it cannot be enclitic: and εἰ σοὶ appears more correct than εἴ σοι which other texts have.

912. κέπφε] Cf. *Pac.* 1067 καὶ κέπφοι τρήρωνες ἀλωπεκιδεῦσι μάχεσθε. The Scholiast here tells us how silly the κέπφος is, and how it lets itself be enticed by foam thrown before it. It is first described as ὄρνεον ἄφρον ὅπερ φιλεῖ θαλάττιον ἀφρὸν ἐσθίειν.

914. τὸ μὲν οὖν β.] No: to interfere (πολυπραγμονεῖν) isn't doing good : but to help the law is, and so is not to suffer any one to commit offence.

916. οὔκουν κ.τ.λ.] Well : but are not the δικασταί on purpose for this duty? Meineke doubts the correctness of καθίστησιν ἄρχειν, and would read ἀρχήν.

919. ὥστ' εἰς ἐμ' ἥκει] The informer is (he concludes) as he professed, ἐπιμελητής of all state matters. ὥστε 'so that, and so' appears perfectly right : Meineke's ὡς is no improvement.

920. προστάτην] Cf. *Pac.* 684 αὐτῷ πονηρὸν προστάτην ἐπεγράψατο. Every μέτοικος at Athens must have a προστάτης, 'a patron or protector.'

923. διατριβή] The man's 'occupation' is gone, if he cannot continue informer. No other life is worth living. The informer in the *Birds* (l. 1451) has much the same spirit. He and his grandfather before him have driven this trade, and he will not 'disgrace his family.'

924. μεταμάθοις] A good example of this word is in Plat. *Rep.* 413 A, where it is said that 'a false opinion departs voluntarily from one who learns better (τοῦ μεταμανθάνοντος).'

925. Βάττου σ.] Battus founded Cyrene : silphium abounded there. And on Cyrenian coins Battus was represented holding this plant. 'Battus' silphium' appears to have passed into a proverb for something rich and rare. *Laserpicium* is the Latin for the plant : and Catullus speaks of 'laserpiciferae Cyrenae.'

926. κατάθου] The best arrangement seems to be to give this to Δίκαιος, then οὗτος, σοὶ λέγει and ταῦτα—λέγει to Carion. The informer does not at first understand that he can be called upon to strip, and in l. 928 dares any one to approach.

929. οὔκουν κ.τ.λ.] Cleverly mocking the informer's words : see above l. 918.

930. μεθ' ἡμέραν] By night such stripping was not uncommon, especially at Athens. Cf. *Ran.* 715.

932. ὁρᾷς] Addressed to his witness.

935. δὸς σύ] To the just man, or to the slave who is carrying his doublet.

938—40. ἔπειτα κ.τ.λ.] They can't be better placed than on a rogue like this : Plutus himself deserves better raiment.

941. ἐμβαδίοις] i.e. the just man's shoes. The informer is to serve as a post on which to nail up the offering.

946. καὶ σύκινον] 'Some helper and fellow of my own grain,' which he expresses by σύκινος 'of fig-wood,' without meaning to reproach his own trade of συκοφάντης, of which he is proud. If however we take κἂν σύκινον (with Meineke and others) it will be 'even of fig wood,' i.e. 'weak, of no great worth ;' for the wood of the fig-tree was all but useless, and σύκινοι ἄνδρες in Theocr. X. 45 is a term of reproach. And then there would be no reference meant by the συκοφάντης to his own trade; though the audience might so apply it. There seems to be an intentional alliteration or similarity of beginning in σύζυγον καὶ σύκινον, which is perhaps better with the old reading καί. In *Ach.* 180 men are described as πρίνινοι and σφενδάμνινοι to express toughness.

948. καταλύει τὴν δ.] A charge readily listened to at Athens. The informer may almost be supposed to be quoting from one of his former speeches.

952. βαλανεῖον] Thither the beggars resorted : of whose ragged choir the informer in his newly-donned garments was fit to be first fiddle. But even there he will not be tolerated.

959—1094. Carion with the just man and the informer being gone, the Chorus remain. They probably sang an interlude after l. 958 in the first edition of the play. An old woman then enters, complaining that she has lost her young lover, who used to court her when she was rich and he was poor. Now things are changed by Plutus' recovery of sight. While she and Chremylus (who has come out to her) are talking, the young man comes in, and jeers at her, Chremylus pretending sympathy but joining in the ridicule. They then enter the house.

960. νέου] 'New' because of his newly-recovered sight.

963. μειρακίσκη] In ridicule : as is ὡρικῶς: which certainly means 'like a young girl, in the fashion of sweet seventeen.' Cf. *Ach.* 272 ὡρικὴν ὑληφόρον. The age meant by μεῖραξ was from fourteen to twenty-one. Of course the old woman acts and speaks in imitation of a young girl.

965. μὴ δῆτ'] No need to call : for Chremylus hearing the arrival comes out.

970. καὶ σύ] The last visitor was a συκοφάντης : so Chremylus thinks this may be another of the same breed but of opposite sex.

972. ἀλλ' οὐ κ.τ.λ.] The courts of law in which the δικασταὶ presided were inscribed with certain letters; and each δικαστὴς drew lots for his special court. To this there is allusion in l. 277 and l. 1167 of this play. It was a heavily punishable offence to sit as dicast when not allotted (οὐ λαχών). But here for ἐδίκαζες, or for ἔκρινες, is put ἔπινες. And in feasts the order of drinking was also settled by lot, perhaps by some drawing of letters. Hence the whole meaning will be 'Did you drink without having duly drawn the lot according to your letter?' i.e. 'Did you drink out of turn?' Chremylus means to mock at the old woman as a tippler. Her appearance no doubt suggested this : she was probably fat and bloated : cf. below l. 1037. So when she denies being an informer, he thinks 'Oh! you have been a wretched old tippler, who used not to drink fair but take too much, and now you have lost your money and blame Plutus.' To which she answers that it is not so, she is anything but fat, she is wasted and pining.

979. ταὐτὰ πάνθ'] γ' αὖ τὰ πάνθ' Holden, which is perhaps better. The MSS. have πάντα ταῦθ' or ταῦτα πάνθ'.

982. ἄν] Expressing habit : very common in Aristophanes esp. with imperfect.

987. οὐ πολλὰ κ.τ.λ.] Ironical. A very modest beggar was your lover ! If (as may be gathered from Lucian) ὑποδήματα were purchaseable for two drachmae, the sums mentioned may be large for their purpose.

989. μισητίας] This must certainly mean 'greediness' here : the other meaning given in L. and S. 'passionate lust' makes no sense. And in *Av.* 1620 μὴ ἀποδιδῷ μισητίᾳ, it is of one who, having promised an offering to the gods, does not pay it 'through greediness, stinginess.' Even the little that my lover did ask (says the doating old woman) he asked not from a wish to get all he could out of me, but from love, wishing for keepsakes.

992. ἐκνομιώτατα] Chremylus takes her very word, see l. 981.

994. πάνυ] Meineke objects to πολὺ...πάνυ and proposes πολὺ μεθέστηκεν, πολύ.

995. τουτονί] It had been sent back to her, and so she had it with her.

999. ἄμητα] εἶδος πλακοῦντος γαλακτώδους. Schol. Perhaps richer and better than her πλακοῦς: it was to show that he did not now want her gifts being himself rich.

1002. πάλαι κ.τ.λ.] A proverb of any who are past their prime. 'The Milesians were stout fellows in their day :' and you were a beauty doubtless, but are so no more. The Scholiast tells us how the Milesians lost their former fame : also that the line was given by the oracle as an answer, when the god was consulted whether the Milesians should be called in as allies. There may be an allusion to this proverb in *Vesp.* 1060—3.

1003. μοχθηρὸs] 'Not a bad sort of fellow,' a man of some sense and taste, not to take such an old frump for choice.

1004. ἔπειτα] To this word Dobree, Meineke, and others, object. Holden says that if ἔπειτα is right, it must mean ' And so, since things are thus, or since he is of this character.' Not a very natural sense for ἔπειτα. It seems rather to mean ' later on, afterwards,' and to be contrasted with πρὸ τοῦ of the next line: nor, had πρὸ τοῦ or πρὸ τοῦ μὲν been followed by ἔπειτα, would there have been any difficulty. The past tense ἦν may account for ἔπειτα. ' Plainly he was all along (in the past time) no fool—he took this old woman from necessity, not from choice—and now afterwards having become rich he no longer contents himself with common fare, whereas before he would eat anything.' Meineke reads ἐπεὶ ξα-πλουτῶν.

1008. ἐκφοράν;] As in Eur. *Alc.* 422 ἀλλ' ἐκφορὰν γὰρ τοῦδε θήσομαι νεκροῦ. The old woman is only fit for burying: cf. *Vesp.* 1365 ὡραίας σοροῦ of an old person. Nearly the same rejoinder is made in *Eccles.* 926 οὐκοῦν ἐπ' ἐκφοράν γε.

1011. φάβιον] βάτιον MSS. Bentley corrected to φάττιον, Meineke to φάβιον which means the same, being a diminutive from φάψ, φαβός. The metrical objection to φάττιον is that there would be a tribrach followed by an anapaest. But it must be owned that many passages have to be altered to establish the canon that anapaest never follows dactyl or tribrach.

1013. μυστηρίοις κ.τ.λ.] A proof of his love was his jealousy. Nay, says Chremylus, he wanted to keep your gifts to himself.

1020. ὄξειν τε τῆς χ.] 'that there was a sweet smell from my skin.' ὄξειν is impersonal, as in *Pac.* 529, *Vesp.* 7059, where a second genitive is added to define the smell.

1021. ἐνέχεις] ἐνέχεες from ἐγχέω. Thasian wine was noted for goodness and perfume.

1026. βοηθεῖν τοῖς ἀδ.] Professions of 'righting the wronged' were often made for their country by Athenian orators. Dobree thinks this verse to be a sneer at such claims. Cf. Isoc. *Panegyr.* p. 51, Demosth. *pro Rhod.* p. 115.

1027. τί γὰρ ποιήσῃ;] 'Quid faciat?' the subjunctive is plainly better than ποιήσει.

1029. ἀντευποιεῖν] In Plato's *Gorgias* p. 520 occur ἀντευποιεῖν and ἀντευπείσεται, but some editors write them *divisim.*

1033. οὐκέτι ζῆν] See above, where her lover is supposed to go to her house for her funeral.

1036. διὰ δακτυλίου] A sort of proverb for thinness. The ring must be as big as the hoop of a sieve, says Chremylus. τηλία appears to have several meanings: but it must here be something circular. It is a flat board in *Vesp.* 147, with which the hole of the chimney is stopped.

L. of C.

1040. φαίνεται] This line well shows the difference between ἔοικε and φαίνεται.

1042. τί φησιν;] σέ φησιν Meineke: but probably σέ φησιν cannot be put for σὲ λέγει, 'he means you.' And as ἀσπάζομαι can hardly be without its acc. case, ἀρχαίαν φίλην seems preferable to ἀρχαία φίλη. The old woman breaks in before the young man can complete his greeting.

1046. ποίου] Indignant astonishment : 'after a long time indeed ! when he was with me yesterday !' I see no objection whatever to the text : χρόνου with διά means 'a long time,' as it also does in the phrase χρόνῳ: e.g. ὡς χρόνῳ ἦλθες, 'how late you come !' Meineke proposes πόσου or πολλοῦ. The first would ask seriously (as in *Ach.* 83 which is referred to) how long the time was. The second would have to be taken as an ironical question ; but without some particles would not be a natural phrase.

1050. πρεσβυτικοί] Rather of a comic style for γεραίτεροι. As the Scholiast says οἰκεῖον τῇ γραΐ λέγει τοῦτο· καὶ γὰρ γέροντες γέρουσιν ἁρμόζουσιν.

1051. ῥυτίδων ὅσας] Cf. 1. 694 τῆς ἀθάρης πολλήν.

1053. λάβῃ] βάλῃ is preferred by Meineke and Holden.

1054. εἰρεσιώνην] Cf. *Eq.* 729, and the note. An old εἰρεσιώνη would be dry and quick to burn.

1056. κάρυα] Above at l. 816 the same kind of game is mentioned. The player would here have to guess πόσα κάρυα, for which is substituted πόσους ὀδόντας in ridicule. Chremylus thinks he can make a pretty good guess ; but he fails, and is called on to pay forfeit.

1061. πλυνόν] 'a wash-pit or wash-tub.' To make a person a πλυνός is to put into him or throw over him everything foul and abusive. So in Psalm lx. 10 'Moab is my wash-pot.' The Scholiast says that πλυνός oxytone is the vessel, πλύνος paroxytone the thing washed. Of this there is no proof; and the explanation of πλυνὸν ποιεῖν given above appears satisfactory. The use of πλύνειν, 'to deluge, souse,' in *Ach.* 381, appears different. To 'make into a wash-tub' and 'to wash' are not the same. You dirty the wash-tub : you clean the clothes. But the very mention of a washing-tub suggests to the young man that the old crone wants a washing and cleaning.

1063. καπηλικῶς] She is well made up, like wares at a shop. κάπηλοι were proverbially dishonest and tricky in giving to poor goods an outward semblance of worth.

1066. οὐχ ὑγ.] You, though old, are as mad as the other man. Or, 'you, as being old, are crazy.' As Dogberry says of Verges, 'An old man, sir, and his wits are not...as I would desire they were.'

1071. ἀλλ' ὦ κ.τ.λ.] Chremylus shows interest in the woman : so the young man says he will give her up to him, in respect for his age.

1089. οὓς ἔχω] ὡς ἔχω Meineke and Holden from MS. Rav. comparing *Eq.* 448.

1090. ἐγὼ δέ γ'] The old woman finds reason to consult Plutus also : then the young man hangs back ; but Chremylus encourages him to enter.

1096. λεπάς] Like a limpet sticks to a rock, so does she to the youth.

1097—1170. Carion hearing a knock comes out, and finds Hermes at the door ; who at first delivers a threat of severe punishment from Zeus for the loss to the gods caused by Plutus' recovery of sight. Carion tells him the gods are rightly served : and Hermes, after bemoaning his former good things, soon turns to make conditions for himself. He will abandon the gods, and take service with Plutus and Chremylus, as presider over athletic contests.

1099. κλαυσιᾷ] This verb appears to belong to the class of which ὀφθαλμιᾶν, λοφᾶν, σιβυλλιᾶν, μαθητιᾶν are instances. They denote a disease or sick craving for something. Cf. *Nub.* 183 μαθητιῶ 'I have a disciple-fever on me, a diseased craving to be a pupil:' and *Eq.* 61 ὁδὲ γέρων σιβυλλιᾷ. The Scholiast says ὅταν ὑπ' ἀνέμου κινῆται ἡ θύρα καὶ ἦχον τινὰ ἐκ τούτου ἀποτελῇ ὁ τοιοῦτος ἦχος ἢ τρισμὸς κλαυσιᾶν λέγεται. Eustathius also notices this use of the word saying ἐπεὶ δοκοῦσι τὰ τοιαῦτα θυρία ἐθέλειν κλαίειν ὡσεὶ νεογιλὰ σκυλάκια. This is surely enough to prove that the word is used of the sound of a door. 'The door has a whining fit, making a noise for nothing.' The form κλαυσίαω therefore is not exactly equivalent to κλαυσείω desiderative ; nor is it very good sense, 'wants to weep,' i. e. 'wants to get itself beaten, shall suffer for it,' as L. and S., Meineke and Holden explain. Aristophanes could (and surely would) have written κλαύσεται if he meant that. Carion comes out, does not see Hermes, who, true to his character, cannot even knock at a door without hiding himself and denying it. Therefore he concludes that the door possessed by a whining fit creaked noisily for nothing.

σέ τοι] Carion is retiring, but Hermes hails him.

1105. εἶτα] The list ends comically : they are all humorously invited to 'come and be killed' like the ducks in the nursery rhyme.

1108. συγκυκήσας] They are to be mixed up somewhat as War's victims in *Pac.* 246 ὡς ἐπιτετρίψεσθ' αὐτίκα ἀπαξάπαντα καταμεμυττωτευμένα.

1110. ἡ γλῶττα κ.τ.λ.] The tongue of victims was cut apart and reserved, as is seen from *Pac.* 1060, *Av.* 1704. It was given to Hermes in his character of herald, the Scholiast says. To this there is allusion ; but the words also express a threat that for his ill news he deserved to have his tongue cut out.

1111. τιὴ δή] Vulg. διὰ τί δή. The MSS. vary : the text above is Meineke's, proposed in the *Vindiciae*, and accepted by Holden.

1115. οὐδεέν] See above l. 138.

1119. σωφρονεῖς] You are very wise in caring for yourself more than for others. Meineke would prefer σωφρονῶν 'quae usitata Aristophani syntaxis est.' But surely the participle would then link itself naturally to ἀπόλωλα κἀπιτέτριμμαι, and Hermes was not pronounced 'wise' for being ruined. Nor in syntax is σωφρονῶν a natural sequence to τῶν ἄλλων θεῶν οὐδέν μοι μέλει, but σωφρονεῖς is. Had the participle been used, it would have been σωφρονοῦντί γε immediately after μέλει μοι; but the interposition of ἐγὼ δ᾽ ἀπόλωλα makes a difference, and therefore σωφρονεῖς is used.

1120. καπηλίσιν] Being dishonest, these fee the god of knavery.

1121. οἰνοῦτταν] Compare μελιτοῦττα from μέλι.

1123. ἀναβάδην] Cf. *Ach.* 399 where Euripides writes plays ἀναβάδην 'upstairs, in a garret.'

1124. ζημίαν] Sometimes the rogues whom you helped were detected and punished.

1126. τετράδι] The fourth day of the month was sacred to Hermes.

πεπεμμένου] 'baked,' from πέπτω (πέσσω, πέττω), as is plain from l. 1142 εὖ πεπεμμένος. Meineke refers it to πέμπω 'for the cakes were not baked on the day when they were offered, but on the day before.' How does he know that? Hermes may have liked hot cakes.

1127. ποθεῖς κ.τ.λ.] Hercules in his search for Hylas heard a voice in the air say this. Hence it passed into a proverb.

1129. ἀσκωλίαζ᾽] At the ἀσκώλια, a day of the Dionysia, they leapt upon wineskins. Cf. Virg. *Georg.* II. 380 'unctos saluere per utres.' Of course a pun on κωλῆς is here intended: probably some such meaning as 'do (or dance) without the ham out there in the cold.' For πρὸς τὴν αἰθρ. cf. *Thesm.* 1001 ἐνταῦθα νῦν οἴμωζε πρὸς τὴν αἰθρίαν.

1131. ὀδύνη κ.τ.λ.] Hermes had lamented the loss of the σπλάγχνα of victims. Carion says he seems to have a kind of pain about the σπλάγχνα, i.e. his own (Hermes') σπλάγχνα. It is told of an English wit that, being bidden to take a morning walk on an empty stomach, he asked his doctor 'on whose?' Cf. *Thesm.* 484 στρόφος μ᾽ ἔχει τὴν γαστέρ᾽, ὦνερ, κὠδύνη. The readings vary in this line between πρὸς and περί: and ἔοικ᾽ ἐπιστρέφειν is in some editions: ἔοικ᾽ ἔτι στρέφειν Meineke.

1132. ἴσον ἴσῳ] Half wine, half water—an unusually strong mixture. In *Eq.* 1187 we have ἔχε καὶ πιεῖν κεκραμένον τρία καὶ δύο. In *Ach.* 354 there is allusion to the half-and-half mixture.

1133. ταύτην...φθάνοις] 'Drink this and get you gone at once.' Plainly Carion gives him a draught of wine to get rid of him: he does not (as some interpret) insult him, for throughout the scene he good-naturedly laughs at him, and in the end admits him as one of the household.

1137. νεανικὸν] Cf. Eur. *Hipp.* 1204 φόβος νεανικός. Plato couples this adjective with καλὸς and γενναῖος, Demosthenes with μέγα.

1138. ἐκφορά] It is plain from the Scholiasts that some read this ἔκφορα n. pl. from ἔκφορος. It also appears that at some sacrifices 'a carrying away' of meats was allowed, at some not so. Notice the different sense of ἐκφορά here and above l. 1008; though it is possible that in l. 1008 this sense may be also alluded to.

1139. καὶ μὴν κ.τ.λ.] 'I helped you to thieve.' 'But you went shares.'

1141. ἐφ' ᾧ τε] Holden is inclined to take ἐφ' ᾧ γε from two MSS, as there can be found authority for ἐφ' ᾧ in the sense 'on condition that.' But ἐφ' ᾧ τε is far commoner: and γε, though suitable, is not necessary, especially as γε occurs in Hermes' next line.

1143. κατήσθιες] As the priest of Aesculapius did: cf. l. 579.

1146. μὴ μνησικακήσῃς] 'Do not bring up old scores, bear a grudge, now that you have got Phyle.' Having succeeded, and being rich, you can afford to be generous. Phyle, a fortress on the confines of Attica and Boeotia, was taken by Thrasybulus, in the time of the thirty tyrants. When the republic was restored at Athens, an amnesty followed, of which Xenophon says ὀμόσαντες ὅρκους ἦ μὴν μὴ μνησικακήσειν, ἔτι καὶ νῦν ὁμοῦ τε πολιτεύονται, καὶ τοῖς ὅρκοις ἔμμενει ὁ δῆμος. *Hellen.* II. 43. The date of this was B.C. 403. The allusion proves this passage to be from the second *Plutus* of B.C. 388, not the first *Plutus* of B. C. 408.

1150. ταὐτομολεῖν] To desert would be accounted shameful. Nicias in the *Knights* l. 21—26, when proposing desertion to Demosthenes, does it in a roundabout way, as hardly venturing on such a word openly.

1151. πατρὶς κ.τ.λ.] Plainly a quotation, perhaps from Euripides. The sentiment in one shape or other occurs often: ἅπασα δὲ χθὼν ἀνδρὶ γενναίῳ πατρίς, Eur. *Fr.*, which Ovid repeats 'omne solum forti patria est.' 'All places that the eye of heaven visits Are to the wise man fair and happy havens.' Shakspeare. There is an utilitarian flavour about Hermes' line which suits with his character. Cicero *Tusc. Disp.* v. 37 gives as an exclamation of Teucer 'Patria est, ubicunque est bene' which looks like a translation of our line: another of Euripides is also quoted on that passage: ὡς πανταχοῦ γε πατρὶς ἡ βόσκουσα γῆ.

1153. στροφαῖον] Presiding over the hinge (στρόφιγξ) of the door. In this character Hermes was set up at the entrance of a house, to watch that no mischievous persons entered, being a thief set to catch a thief. But Carion, taking the word as 'god of turns and tricks,' says 'we don't want any στροφαὶ now.'

1157. παλιγκάπηλον] Used figuratively by Demosthenes *c. Arist* 784 παλιγκάπηλος πονηρίας. We (says Carion), being rich, do not want to make profit by petty traffic. Still less do we want a patron of knavery (δόλιος).

1159. ἡγεμόνιον] Hermes was ἐνόδιος and πομπαῖος, a shower of the way both to living and dead.

1161. ἐναγώνιος] ἐπιστάτης τῶν ἀγώνων Schol.

1163. μουσικοὺς κ. γ.] Meineke would prefer μουσικῆς, for which change there seems no reason. He also thinks some lines have been lost. As Holden remarks, l. 1126 does not plainly concern anything that Hermes has said.

1166. οὐκ ἐτὸς κ.τ.λ.] Dicasts may well like to have their names entered on several juries, that they may be sure of having cases to try and fees to receive. See above on l. 277 and l. 972. And Hermes by being jack of so many trades has secured himself a pittance.

1168. ἐπὶ τούτοις] 'On these terms,' of being ἐναγώνιος; but the connexion is not very plain : nor yet has the διακονικὸς of next line any reference to ἐναγώνιος.

1170. διακονικὸς] Hermes had wanted to enter their service, to be ξύνοικος with them. He is the servant, the menial of the gods: esp. in Aristophanes does he appear in this character; therefore, when he has got a footing as ἐναγώνιος, Carion says, if he is to be διάκονος of any sort, he must 'show himself διακονικός.'

1171—1209. The priest of Zeus the Preserver complains that his gains are gone : no more sacrifices: no more perquisites. He proposes to become priest of Plutus, who is, says Chremylus, the true Zeus the Preserver. They prepare to inaugurate the new worship with torches and pitchers, and go out in procession, the Chorus bringing up the rear.

1172. τί γὰρ ἀλλ' ἢ κακῶς] The adverb does not answer the question τί ἔστιν very suitably: we should expect either a noun, as in *Ran.* 437 τουτὶ τί ἦν τὸ πρᾶγμα ἀλλ' ἢ Διὸς Κόρινθος, or a verb is expressed in the answer, as in *Eccl.* 769 φυλάξομαι πρὶν ἄν γ' ἴδω τὸ πλῆθος ὅ τι βουλεύεται. A. τί γὰρ ἄλλο γ' ἢ φέρειν παρεσκευασμένοι τὰ πράγματ' εἰσίν; Hence A. de Velsen would omit the next line (which in the MSS. is imperfect), so that τί γὰρ ἀλλ' ἢ κακῶς ἀπόλωλα may be connected. Holden proposes to read l. 1173 ἀφ' οὗπερ ὁ Πλοῦτος οὗτος (or αὖθις) ἤρξατο βλέπειν, connecting τί γὰρ...ἀπόλωλα.

1178. εἰσὶ πλούσιοι] And therefore they have nothing to be 'saved' from, riches being the only thing worth coveting, poverty the only danger worth escaping.

1180. ὁ δέ τις ἄν] Repeat ἔθυσεν.

1181. ἐκαλλιερεῖτο] The active voice is generally used in Xenophon and prose writers. The Scholiast says here ἑόρταζεν ἐν τῷ οἴκῳ. Sacrifices were always attended with feasting; but the historians use καλλιερεῖν of a king or general offering public sacrifice and obtaining good omens.

1186. καὐτός] I too, like his worshippers, shall bid farewell to Zeus.

1189. ὁ Ζεύς] Plutus of course is the Preserver: 'regina pecunia.' Hor.

1191. ἱδρυσόμεθ'] So the goddess Peace is solemnly enthroned with inaugural rites. Cf. *Pac.* 922 sqq.

1193. τὸν ὀπισθόδομον] The public treasury was behind the Parthenon.

1194. ἐκδότω] 'bring out from the house.'

1197. ἐγὼ δέ] The old woman fears she will be left out in the cold, but an occupation is found for her. For the use of χύτραι in an inauguration cf. *Pac.* 922 ταύτην χύτραις ἱδρυτέον.

1199. ποικίλα] πορφυροῖς γὰρ καὶ ποικίλοις ἱματίοις ἐπόμπευον. Schol. And the old woman of her own vanity (αὐτή) had come gaudily dressed.

1205. ταῖς μὲν ἄλλαις κ.τ.λ.] 'Commonly the mother (lees, sediment) is on the pots, here the pots are on the mother.' The meaning of 'mother' is near enough to γραῦς 'scum' to give a fair equivalent pun.

1207. ἐπιπολῆς] Cf. *Eccles.* 1108 ἐπιπολῆς τοῦ σήματος.

INDEX.

CAMBRIDGE: PRINTED BY C. J. CLAY, M.A. AND SONS, AT THE UNIVERSITY PRESS.

CAMBRIDGE UNIVERSITY PRESS.

THE PITT PRESS SERIES.

*** *Complete catalogues of the Pitt Press Series and of the other publications of the University Press will be sent on application.*

*** *Many of the books in this list can be had in two volumes, Text and Notes separately.*

I. GREEK.

Aristophanes. Aves—Plutus—Ranæ. By W. C. GREEN, M.A., late Assistant Master at Rugby School. 3*s*. 6*d*. each.
—— **Vespae.** By C. E. GRAVES, M.A. 3*s*. 6*d*.
Aristotle. Outlines of the Philosophy of. By EDWIN WALLACE, M.A., LL.D. Third Edition, Enlarged. 4*s*. 6*d*.
Euripides. Alcestis. By W. S. HADLEY, M.A. [*In the Press.*
—— **Heracleidae.** By E. A. BECK, M.A., and C. E. S. HEADLAM, M.A. 3*s*. 6*d*.
—— **Hercules Furens.** By A. GRAY, M.A., and J. T. HUTCHINSON, M.A. 2*s*.
—— **Hippolytus.** By W. S. HADLEY, M.A. 2*s*.
—— **Iphigeneia in Aulis.** By C. E. S. HEADLAM, M.A. 2*s*. 6*d*.
—— **Hecuba.** By W. S. HADLEY, M.A. 2*s*. 6*d*.
—— **Orestes.** By N. WEDD, M.A. [*In the Press.*
Herodotus, Book V. By E. S. SHUCKBURGH, M.A. 3*s*.
—— **Books VI., VIII., IX.** By the same Editor. 4*s*. each.
—— **Book VIII. Ch. 1—90. Book IX. Ch. 1—89.** By the same Editor. 2*s*. 6*d*. each.
Homer. Odyssey, Book IX. By G. M. EDWARDS, M.A. 2*s*. 6*d*. **Book X.** By the same Editor. 2*s*. 6*d*. **Book XXI.** By the same Editor. 2*s*.
—— **Iliad. Bks. VI., XXII., XXIII., XXIV.** By the same Editor. 2*s*. each.
Platonis Apologia Socratis. By J. ADAM, M.A. 3*s*. 6*d*.
—— **Crito.** By the same Editor. 2*s*. 6*d*.
—— **Euthyphro.** By the same Editor. 2*s*. 6*d*.
—— **Protagoras.** By J. & A. M. ADAM. 4*s*. 6*d*.
Sophocles. Oedipus Tyrannus. School Edition. By R. C. JEBB, Litt.D., LL.D. 4*s*. 6*d*.
Thucydides. Book III. With Introduction and Notes. By A. W. SPRATT, M.A. [*Nearly ready.*
—— **Book VII.** By H. A. HOLDEN, M.A., LL.D. 5*s*.
Xenophon. Agesilaus. By H. HAILSTONE, M.A. 2*s*. 6*d*.
—— **Anabasis.** By A. PRETOR, M.A. Two vols. 7*s*. 6*d*.
—— **Books I. and II.** By the same. 4*s*.
—— **Books I. III. IV. and V.** By the same. 2*s*. each.
—— **Books II. VI. and VII.** By the same. 2*s*. 6*d*. each.
Xenophon. Cyropaedeia. Books I. II. By Rev. H. A. HOLDEN, M.A., LL.D. 2 vols. 6*s*.
—— —— **Books III. IV. and V.** By the same Editor. 5*s*.
—— —— **Books VI. VII. VIII.** By the same Editor. 5*s*.

London: Cambridge Warehouse, Ave Maria Lane.

II. LATIN.

Beda's Ecclesiastical History, Books III., IV. By J. E. B.
MAYOR, M.A., and J. R. LUMBY, D.D. Revised Edition. 7s. 6d.
—— **Books I. II.** [*In the Press.*

Caesar. De Bello Gallico, Comment. I. By A. G. PESKETT,
M.A., Fellow of Magdalene College, Cambridge. 1s. 6d. COMMENT. II.
III. 2s. COMMENT. I. II. III. 3s. COMMENT. IV. and V. 1s. 6d. COMMENT.
VII. 2s. COMMENT. VI. and COMMENT. VIII. 1s. 6d. each.
—— **De Bello Civili, Comment. I.** By the same Editor. 3s.
—— —— **Com. III.** By the same. [*In the Press.*

Cicero. De Amicitia.—De Senectute. By J. S. REID, Litt.D.,
Fellow of Gonville and Caius College. 3s. 6d. each.
—— **In Verrem Actio Prima.** By H. COWIE, M.A. 1s. 6d.
—— **In Q. Caecilium Divinatio et in C. Verrem Actio.**
By W. E. HEITLAND, M.A., and H. COWIE, M.A. 3s.
—— **Philippica Secunda.** By A. G. PESKETT, M.A. 3s. 6d.
—— **Oratio pro Archia Poeta.** By J. S. REID, Litt.D. 2s.
—— **Pro L. Cornelio Balbo Oratio.** By the same. 1s. 6d.
—— **Oratio pro Milone.** New Edition. By J. S. REID,
Litt.D. 2s. 6d.
—— **Oratio pro L. Murena.** By W. E. HEITLAND, M.A. 3s.
—— **Pro Cn. Plancio Oratio,** by H. A. HOLDEN, LL.D. 4s. 6d.
—— **Pro P. Cornelio Sulla.** By J. S. REID, Litt.D. 3s. 6d.

Cornelius Nepos. Lives of Miltiades, Themistocles,
Aristides, Pausanias and Cimon, by E. S. SHUCKBURGH, M.A. 1s. 6d.

Horace. Epistles, Book I. By E. S. SHUCKBURGH, M.A. 2s. 6d.
—— **Odes and Epodes.** By J. GOW, Litt.D. [*In the Press.*

Livy. Books IV, VI, IX, XXVII. By H. M. STEPHENSON,
M.A. 2s. 6d. each.
—— **Book V.** By L. WHIBLEY, M.A. 2s. 6d.
—— **Bks. XXI, XXII.** By M. S. DIMSDALE, M.A. 2s. 6d. each.

Lucretius. Book V. By J. D. DUFF, M.A. 2s.

Ovidii Nasonis Fastorum Liber VI. By A. SIDGWICK, M.A.,
1s. 6d.

Plautus. Epidicus. By J. H. GRAY, M.A. 3s.
—— **Asinaria.** By the same Editor. 3s. 6d.
—— **Stichus.** By C. A. M. FENNELL, Litt.D. 2s. 6d.

Tacitus. Agricola and Germania. By H. M. STEPHENSON,
M.A. 3s.

Terence. Hautontimorumenos. By J. H. GRAY, M.A. 3s.

Vergili Maronis Aeneidos Libri I.—XII. By A. SIDGWICK,
M.A. 1s. 6d. each.
—— **Bucolica.** By the same Editor. 1s. 6d.
—— **Georgicon Libri I. II.** By the same Editor. 2s.
—— —— **Libri III. IV.** By the same Editor. 2s.
—— **The Complete Works.** By the same Editor. Two vols.
Vol. I. containing the Introduction and Text. 3s. 6d. Vol. II. The Notes. 4s. 6d.

III. FRENCH.

Corneille. Polyeucte. By E. G.W. BRAUNHOLTZ, M.A., Ph. D. 2*s.*

De Bonnechose. Lazare Hoche. By C. COLBECK, M.A.
Revised Edition. Four Maps. 2*s.*

Delavigne. Louis XI. Edited by H. W. EVE, M.A. 2*s.*

De Lamartine. Jeanne D'Arc. By Rev. A. C. CLAPIN,
M.A. New edition revised, by A. R. ROPES, M.A. 1*s.* 6*d.*

De Vigny. La Canne de Jonc. By H. W. EVE, M.A. 1*s.* 6*d.*

Erckmann-Chatrian. La Guerre. By Rev. A. C. CLAPIN,
M.A. 3*s.*

Guizot. Discours sur l'histoire de la Révolution d'Angleterre.
By H. W. EVE, M.A. 2*s.* 6*d.*

Merimée. Colomba. Edited by A. R. ROPES, M.A. 2*s.*

Molière. Le Bourgeois Gentilhomme, Comédie-Ballet en
Cinq Actes. (1670.) By Rev. A. C. CLAPIN, M.A. Revised Edition. 1*s.* 6*d.*

—— **L'École des Femmes.** By G. SAINTSBURY, M.A. 2*s.* 6*d.*

—— **Les Précieuses Ridicules.** By E. G. W. BRAUNHOLTZ,
M.A. 2*s.* **Abridged Edition.** 1*s.*

—— **Le Misanthrope.** By the same Editor. 2*s.* 6*d.*

Piron. La Métromanie. A Comedy. By G. MASSON, B.A. 2*s.*

Ponsard. Charlotte Corday. By A. R. ROPES, M.A. 2*s.*

Racine. Les Plaideurs. By E. G. W. BRAUNHOLTZ, M.A. 2*s.*

—— —— **Abridged Edition.** 1*s.*

Sainte-Beuve. M. Daru (Causeries du Lundi, Vol. IX.).
By G. MASSON, B.A. 2*s.*

Saintine. Picciola. By Rev. A. C. CLAPIN, M.A. 2*s.*

Scribe and Legouvé. Bataille de Dames. By Rev. H. A.
BULL, M.A. 2*s.*

Scribe. Le Verre d'Eau. By C. COLBECK, M.A. 2*s.*

Souvestre. Un Philosophe sous les Toits. By H. W. EVE,
M.A. 2*s.*

—— **Le Serf and Le Chevrier de Lorraine.** Edited by
A. R. ROPES, M.A. 2*s.*

—— **Le Serf.** Edited by A. R. ROPES, M.A., with Vocabu-
lary. 1*s.* 6*d.*

Thierry. Lettres sur l'histoire de France (XIII.—XXIV.).
By G. MASSON, B.A., and G. W. PROTHERO, Litt. D. 2*s.* 6*d.*

Voltaire. Histoire du Siècle de Louis XIV. Chaps. I.—
XIII. By G. MASSON, B.A., and G. W. PROTHERO, Litt. D. 2*s.* 6*d.* PART II.
CHAPS. XIV.—XXIV. 2*s.* 6*d.* PART III. CHAPS. XXV. to end. 2*s.* 6*d.*

Xavier de Maistre. La Jeune Sibérienne. Le Lépreux de
la Cité d'Aoste. By G. MASSON, B.A. 1*s.* 6*d.*

IV. GERMAN.

Ballads on German History. By W. WAGNER, Ph.D. 2s.

Benedix. Doctor Wespe. Lustspiel in fünf Aufzügen. By KARL HERMANN BREUL, M.A., Ph.D. 3s.

German Dactylic Poetry. By WILHELM WAGNER, Ph.D. 3s.

Goethe's Knabenjahre. (1749—1761.) By W. WAGNER, Ph.D. New edition revised and enlarged, by J. W. CARTMELL, M.A. 2s.

—— **Hermann und Dorothea.** By WILHELM WAGNER, Ph.D. New edition revised, by J. W. CARTMELL, M.A. 3s. 6d.

Gutzkow. Zopf und Schwert. Lustspiel in fünf Aufzügen. By H. J. WOLSTENHOLME, B.A. (Lond.). 3s. 6d.

Hackländer. Der geheime Agent. Edited by E. L. MILNER BARRY, M.A. 3s.

Hauff. Das Bild des Kaisers. By KARL HERMANN BREUL, M.A., Ph.D., University Lecturer in German. 3s.

—— **Das Wirthshaus im Spessart.** By the late A. SCHLOTTMANN, Ph.D. and J. W. CARTMELL, M.A. 3s.

—— **Die Karavane.** By A. SCHLOTTMANN, Ph.D. 3s.

Immermann. Der Oberhof. By WILHELM WAGNER, Ph.D. 3s.

Klee. Die deutschen Heldensagen (Hagen und Hilde, and Gudrun). Edited by H. J. WOLSTENHOLME, B.A. (Lond.). 3s.

Kohlrausch. Das Jahr 1813. By WILHELM WAGNER, Ph.D. 2s.

Lessing and Gellert. Selected Fables. By KARL HERMANN BREUL, M.A., Ph.D. 3s.

Mendelssohn's Letters. Selections from. By J. SIME, M.A. 3s.

Raumer. Der erste Kreuzzug (1095—1099). By WILHELM WAGNER, Ph.D. 2s.

Riehl. Culturgeschichtliche Novellen. By H. J. WOLSTEN-HOLME, B.A. (Lond.). 3s. 6d.

—— **Die Ganerben and Die Gerechtigkeit Gottes.** By the same Editor. 3s.

Schiller. Maria Stuart. By KARL HERMANN BREUL, M.A. Ph.D. 3s. 6d.

—— **Wilhelm Tell.** By the same Editor. 2s. 6d. **Abridged Edition.** 1s. 6d.

—— **Geschichte des dreissigjährigen Kriegs.** Buch III. By the same Editor. 3s.

—— **Wallenstein I. (Wallenstein's Lager and Die Picco-** lomini). By the same Editor. 3s. 6d.

—— **Wallenstein II. (Wallenstein's Tod).** By the same Editor. [In the Press.

Uhland. Ernst, Herzog von Schwaben. By H. J. WOLSTEN-HOLME, B.A. 3s. 6d.

V. ENGLISH.

Bacon's History of the Reign of King Henry VII. By the Rev. Professor LUMBY, D.D. 3*s.*

Cowley's Essays. By the same Editor. 4*s.*

Milton's Comus and Arcades. By A. W. VERITY, M.A., sometime Scholar of Trinity College. 3*s.*

Milton's Ode on the Morning of Christ's Nativity, L'Allegro, Il Penseroso and Lycidas. By the same Editor. 2*s.* 6*d.*

Milton's Samson Agonistes. By the same Editor. 2*s.* 6*d.*

—— **Sonnets.** By the same Editor. 1*s.* 6*d.*

Milton's Paradise Lost. Books I. II. By the same Editor. 2*s.*

—— —— **Bks. III. IV.** By the same. 2*s.*

—— —— **Books V. VI.** By the same. 2*s.*

—— —— **Books VII. VIII.** By the same. 2*s.*

—— —— **Books IX. X.** By the same. [*Preparing.*

—— —— **Books XI. XII.** By the same. 2*s.*

More's History of King Richard III. By J. R. LUMBY, D.D. 3*s.* 6*d.*

More's Utopia. By the same Editor. 3*s.* 6*d.*

Scott. Marmion. Edited with Introduction, Notes and Glossary by J. HOWARD B. MASTERMAN, B.A., Lecturer of St John's College, Cambridge. 2*s.* 6*d.*

Shakespeare. A Midsummer Night's Dream. Edited, with Introduction, Notes and Glossary by A. W. VERITY, M.A. 1*s.* 6*d.*

—— **Twelfth Night.** By the same Editor. 1*s.* 6*d.*

—— **Julius Cæsar.** By the same Editor. [*In the Press.*

Sidney, Sir Philip. An Apologie for Poetrie. By E. S. SHUCKBURGH, M.A. The Text is a revision of that of the first edition of 1595. 3*s.*

VI. EDUCATIONAL SCIENCE.

Comenius, John Amos, Bishop of the Moravians. His Life and Educational Works, by S. S. LAURIE, LL.D., F.R.S.E. 3*s.* 6*d.*

Education, Three Lectures on the Practice of. I. On Marking, by H. W. EVE, M.A. II. On Stimulus, by A. SIDGWICK, M.A. III. On the Teaching of Latin Verse Composition, by E. A. ABBOTT, D.D. 2*s.*

Stimulus. A Lecture delivered for the Teachers' Training Syndicate, May, 1882, by A. SIDGWICK, M.A. 1*s.*

Locke on Education. By the Rev. R. H. QUICK, M.A. 3*s.* 6*d.*

Milton's Tractate on Education. A facsimile reprint from the Edition of 1673. By O. BROWNING, M.A. 2*s.*

Modern Languages, Lectures on the Teaching of. By C. COLBECK, M.A. 2*s.*

Teacher, General Aims of the, and Form Management. Two Lectures delivered in the University of Cambridge in the Lent Term, 1883, by F. W. FARRAR, D.D., and R. B. POOLE, B.D. 1*s.* 6*d.*

Teaching, Theory and Practice of. By the Rev. E. THRING, M.A., late Head Master of Uppingham School. New Edition. 4*s.* 6*d.*

London : Cambridge Warehouse, Ave Maria Lane.

VII. MATHEMATICS.

Arithmetic for Schools. By C. SMITH, M.A., Master of
Sidney Sussex College, Cambridge. With or without Answers. Second Edition. 3s. 6d. Or in two Parts. 2s. each.

Key to Smith's Arithmetic. By G. HALE, M.A. 7s. 6d.

Elementary Algebra. By W. W. ROUSE BALL, M.A., Fellow
and Tutor of Trinity College, Cambridge. 4s. 6d.

Euclid's Elements of Geometry. By H. M. TAYLOR, M.A.,
Fellow and formerly Tutor of Trinity College, Cambridge.

Books I.—VI. 4s. **Books I.—IV.** 3s. **Books I. and II.** 1s. 6d.
Books III. and IV. 1s. 6d. **Books V. and VI.** 1s. 6d.
Books XI. and XII. [*In the Press.*

Solutions to the Exercises in Taylor's Euclid, Books I—IV.
By W. W. TAYLOR, M.A. 6s.

Elements of Statics and Dynamics. By S. L. LONEY, M.A.,
late Fellow of Sidney Sussex College, Cambridge. 7s. 6d. Or in two parts.

> **Part I. Elements of Statics.** 4s. 6d.
> **Part II. Elements of Dynamics.** 3s. 6d.

Solutions to the Examples in the Elements of Statics and
Dynamics. By the same Author. 7s. 6d.

Mechanics and Hydrostatics for Beginners. By the same
Author. 4s. 6d.

An Elementary Treatise on Plane Trigonometry. By E.
W. HOBSON, Sc.D., Fellow and Tutor of Christ's College, Cambridge, and
C. M. JESSOP, M.A., late Fellow of Clare College, Cambridge. 4s. 6d.

The Elements of English Grammar. By A. S. WEST, M.A.,
Trinity College, Cambridge. 2s. 6d.

English Grammar for Beginners. By A. S. WEST, M.A. 1s.

British India, a Short History of. By E. S. CARLOS, M.A.,
late Head Master of Exeter Grammar School. 1s.

Geography, Elementary Commercial. A Sketch of the Commodities and the Countries of the World. By H. R. MILL, D.Sc., F.R.S.E.
New Edition Revised and Enlarged. 1s. 6d.

Geography, an Atlas of Commercial. (A Companion to the
above.) By J. G. BARTHOLOMEW, F.R.G.S. With an Introduction by HUGH
ROBERT MILL, D.Sc. 3s.

Other Volumes are in preparation.

London: Cambridge Warehouse, Ave Maria Lane.

𝕿𝖍𝖊 𝕮𝖆𝖒𝖇𝖗𝖎𝖉𝖌𝖊 𝕭𝖎𝖇𝖑𝖊 𝖋𝖔𝖗 𝕾𝖈𝖍𝖔𝖔𝖑𝖘 𝖆𝖓𝖉 𝕮𝖔𝖑𝖑𝖊𝖌𝖊𝖘.

GENERAL EDITORS:

J. J. S. PEROWNE, D.D., BISHOP OF WORCESTER.
A. F. KIRKPATRICK, D.D., REGIUS PROFESSOR OF HEBREW.

Now Ready. Cloth, Extra Fcap. 8vo. With Maps.

Book of Joshua. By Rev. G. F. MACLEAR, D.D.   2s. 6d.
Book of Judges. By Rev. J. J. LIAS, M.A.   3s. 6d.
First and Second Books of Samuel. By Rev. Prof. KIRKPATRICK, D.D.   3s. 6d. each.
First and Second Books of Kings. Prof. LUMBY, D.D.   3s. 6d. each.
Books of Ezra and Nehemiah. By Rev. Prof. RYLE, D.D.   4s. 6d.
Book of Job. By Rev. A. B. DAVIDSON, D.D.   5s.
Psalms. Book I. By Prof. KIRKPATRICK, D.D.   3s. 6d.
Psalms. Books II and III. By the same Editor.   3s. 6d.
Book of Ecclesiastes. By Very Rev. E. H. PLUMPTRE, D.D.   5s.
Book of Jeremiah. By Rev. A. W. STREANE, D.D.   4s. 6d.
Book of Ezekiel. By Rev. A. B. DAVIDSON, D.D.   5s.
Book of Hosea. By Rev. T. K. CHEYNE, M.A., D.D.   3s.
Books of Obadiah & Jonah. By Archdeacon PEROWNE.   2s. 6d.
Book of Micah. By Rev. T. K. CHEYNE, M.A., D.D.   1s. 6d.
Haggai, Zechariah & Malachi. By Archd. PEROWNE.   3s. 6d.
Book of Malachi. By the same Editor.   1s.
Gospel according to St Matthew. By Rev. A. CARR, M.A.   2s. 6d.
Gospel according to St Mark. Rev. G. F. MACLEAR, D.D.   2s. 6d.
Gospel according to St Luke. By the Very Rev. F. W. FARRAR, D.D.   4s. 6d.
Gospel according to St John. By Rev. A. PLUMMER, D.D.   4s. 6d.
Acts of the Apostles. By Rev. Prof. LUMBY, D.D.   4s. 6d.
Epistle to the Romans. By Rev. H. C. G. MOULE, D.D.   3s. 6d.
First and Second Corinthians. By Rev. J. J. LIAS, M.A.   2s. each.
Epistle to the Galatians. By Rev. E. H. PEROWNE, D.D.   1s. 6d.
Epistle to the Ephesians. By Rev. H. C. G. MOULE, D.D.   2s. 6d.
Epistle to the Philippians. By the same Editor.   2s. 6d.
Colossians and Philemon. By the same Editor.   2s.
Epistles to the Thessalonians. By Rev. G. G. FINDLAY, B.A.   2s.
Epistle to the Hebrews. By the Very Rev. F. W. FARRAR, D.D.   3s. 6d.
Epistle of St James. Very Rev. E. H. PLUMPTRE, D.D.   1s. 6d.
Epistles of St Peter and St Jude. By the same Editor.   2s. 6d.
Epistles of St John. By Rev. A. PLUMMER, D.D.   3s. 6d.
Book of Revelation. By the late Rev. W. H. SIMCOX, M.A.   3s.
Epistles to Timothy & Titus. By Rev. A. E. HUMPHREYS, M.A.
[Nearly ready.

The Smaller Cambridge Bible for Schools.

Now ready. Price 1*s. each Volume, with Map.*
Book of Joshua. By J. S. BLACK, M.A.
Book of Judges. By the same Editor.
First Book of Samuel. By Rev. Prof. KIRKPATRICK, D.D.
Second Book of Samuel. By the same Editor.
First Book of Kings. By Rev. Prof. LUMBY, D.D.
Second Book of Kings. By the same Editor.
Gospel according to St Matthew. By Rev. A. CARR, M.A.
Gospel according to St Mark. By Rev. G. F. MACLEAR, D.D.
Gospel according to St Luke. By the Very Rev. F. W. FARRAR, D.D.
Gospel according to St John. By Rev. A. PLUMMER, D.D.
Acts of the Apostles. By Rev. Prof. LUMBY, D.D.

The Cambridge Greek Testament for Schools and Colleges,

with a Revised Text, based on the most recent critical authorities,
and English Notes.

GENERAL EDITOR: J. J. S. PEROWNE, D.D.,
BISHOP OF WORCESTER.

Gospel according to St Matthew. By Rev. A. CARR, M.A.
With 4 Maps. 4*s.* 6*d.*
Gospel according to St Mark. By Rev. G. F. MACLEAR, D.D.
With 3 Maps. 4*s.* 6*d.*
Gospel according to St Luke. By the Very Rev. F. W.
FARRAR, D.D. With 4 Maps. 6*s.*
Gospel according to St John. By Rev. A. PLUMMER, D.D.
With 4 Maps. 6*s.*
Acts of the Apostles. By Rev. Professor LUMBY, D.D.
With 4 Maps. 6*s.*
First Epistle to the Corinthians. By Rev. J. J. LIAS, M.A. 3*s.*
Second Epistle to the Corinthians. By the same Editor. 3*s.*
Epistle to the Hebrews. By the Very Rev. F. W. FARRAR,
D.D. 3*s.* 6*d.*
Epistles of St John. By Rev. A. PLUMMER, D.D. 4*s.*

GENERAL EDITOR: REV. J. A. ROBINSON, B.D.,
NORRISIAN PROFESSOR OF DIVINITY.

Epistle to the Philippians. By Rev. H. C. G. MOULE, D.D.
[*In the Press.*
Epistle of St James. By Rev. A. CARR, M.A. [*In the Press.*
Book of Revelation. By the late Rev. W. H. SIMCOX, M.A. 5*s.*

London: C. J. CLAY AND SONS,
CAMBRIDGE WAREHOUSE, AVE MARIA LANE.
Glasgow: 263, ARGYLE STREET.
Leipzig: F. A. BROCKHAUS.
New York: MACMILLAN AND CO.

CAMBRIDGE: PRINTED BY J. & C. F. CLAY, AT THE UNIVERSITY PRESS.

www.ingramcontent.com/pod-product-compliance
Lightning Source LLC
Chambersburg PA
CBHW031441280326
41927CB00038B/1482